Derek Tangye was educated at Harrow and subsequently worked as a journalist on national newspapers. During the war and afterwards he was a member of MI5, before he and Jeannie moved to Minack.

In addition to the Minack Chronicles, his most recent book was *The World of Minack*, an illustrated anthology of quotations from the Chronicles. He is also the author of *Time Was Mine*, a travel book, and *One King*, a survey of the British Commonwealth, and editor of *Went the Day Well*, a collection of tributes to those killed during the Second World War.

Jean Nicol Tangye was the author of *Meet Me at the Savoy* and the trilogy *Hotel Regina*, *Home is the Hotel* and *Bertioni's Hotel*.

DEREK TANGYE

MONTY'S LEAP

WARNER BOOKS

A *Warner* Book

First published in Great Britain in 1993 by Michael Joseph Ltd
This edition published in 1994 by Warner Books

Copyright © Derek Tangye 1993

The moral right of the author has been asserted

A CIP catalogue record for this book
is available from the British Library

ISBN 0 7515 0751 2

Printed in England by Clays Ltd, St Ives plc

Warner Books
A Division of
Little, Brown and Company (UK) Limited
Brettenham House
Lancaster Place
London WC2E 7EN

To Anne Askwith

List of Illustrations

The Illustrators

Photographs 1, 3, 5, 6, 7, 8, 9 and 10 are by David Wills. Photograph 2 is by Scott Morrish.

The line drawings are by Denise White.

DAVID WILLS

David Wills came from London to live in the far west of Cornwall in 1958 with his wife Joan. His photographs and paintings capture the various moods of the Cornish moors, the sea, the cliffs, their natural beauty and wildlife. These photographs and paintings have been sold worldwide.

SCOTT MORRISH

'I am twenty years old. I live in Ilsington on the edge of Dartmoor. I have studied photography at Plymouth College of Art and Design. While at college I wrote to you because I wanted to meet you, and see Minack, to find out if the sense of purpose you convey in the Chronicles was there for others to experience; and it was.'

DENISE WHITE

'I studied at the Bournmouth and Poole College of Art and Design, and at the Southampton Institute of Higher Education, specializing in illustration. I am twenty-two years old. I came to see you bringing the pastel I had done of Minack because my imagination had been captured by the Minack Chronicles . . . and by Jeannie's illustrations. She has been my inspiration, and I am over the moon that you feel that my work reflects her sensitivity.'

I

Early March.

Penzance Station car park.

I had locked the car four days before, London impending. Now I was unlocking it, London experienced.

I had set off in a confident mood. A mood bolstered by the variety of people who come to Minack. People who come down the long winding lane, stepping across the little stream at Monty's Leap, often nervous.

A husband said to his wife, 'He may shoot at us!'

At that moment a gust of wind whipped a polythene sheet that covered a broken glass frame in the Orlyt greenhouse beside the lane; and it sounded like the crack of a rifle shot.

'My God,' said the husband, 'he *is* shooting at us!'

Stimulating conversations often accompany such visits, conversations of gusto, with an earthy sense of realism, because they are not trivial people who come to Minack. It is too difficult to find, and there are no signposts. There is nothing anaemic about the conversations. They spring from the deep-down experiences of people, people who have to face the everyday reality of survival. They are of all ages, and come from every sphere of life. Children come here, teenagers, and the mood is natural. Difference in age has no meaning. Wavelengths are the secret. One can be on the same wavelength of a ten-year-old, but not of someone of one's own age. Sitting on the porch, I learn more about the way people live, suffer, rejoice, than I could ever learn in a conventional town life.

I had set off, therefore, in a confident mood, a too confident mood.

In retrospect I compare my mood with that of an incident of my schooldays, a similar mood of over-confidence. I had made sixty-three runs for Copthorne, my preparatory school, against a school called The Wick, and I had been awarded my colours after the match.

A few weeks later Copthorne met The Wick again, this time on their home ground. I had been promoted first wicket down, batting star of the team; and when the moment came I sauntered out of the pavilion on a clear day, my newly awarded cap at a jaunty angle, believing myself immortal against anything The Wick could bowl at me.

I was out third ball.

I had been over-confident; and now once again I had been over-confident, as I will soon recall. But now, the experience over, I began to drive away from Penzance Station . . . and I was remembering past scenes.

In the early months of every year I would arrive there in OPA 40, the Land-Rover, boxes of daffodils, anemones and violets packed by Jeannie bulging in the back, to be greeted by my friends like George, Barry and Donald. 'Here comes the Home Farm!' George Mills would call out in jest as I arrived, late as usual, with the flower train about to leave for Paddington. 'Give him priority, stop here, this is your wagon!' And my friends would seize the boxes, and transfer them speedily to the wagon. Wonderful times, of kindness, trust, no greed, with an ability to share, each in our own way, the pleasure, the effort, of sending yet another cargo of flowers to market, so that all of us in different ways could earn our living.

There were other scenes to remember. Jeannie leaving her peasant world behind her, setting off to her other world of the Savoy, the Berkeley, and Claridge's, me waving goodbye, then loping back down the platform towards a period of bachelordom. Then there were the occasions we travelled together; the occasion, for instance, when we had been invited to the first of the Hatchards Authors of the Year receptions and, because Jeannie believed that special occasions should be treated with style, we travelled first class despite the fact that the daffodil season had been a disastrous one. In those days a steam engine, the Cornish Riviera, puffed its way out of Penzance Station at eleven o'clock; and we sat at the table in the restaurant car with a vase of fresh anemones on the table, and Jeannie and I would sip gin and tonic, and toast

each other . . . and flirt. There were other times to
remember: darkness in the station but for a ghostly
light which made the station unreal, when I was
waiting for Jeannie, waiting for her return from
one of her sporadic trips . . . and my impatience
because the train was late, then the greeting, then
the account of her experiences.

Those were memories of my time with Jeannie;
and now there were other scenes to remember.

I was alone, for instance, at the station waiting
for a girl to arrive I did not know. I was standing
at the entrance, half hidden by a pillar, when the
girl who had written to me saying that she wanted
to see Minack, that she was coming from London
just for the day in the hope that she would meet
me, appeared from the throng of passengers stream-
ing out of the train and the station. She did not
know I would be there. I did not know what she
looked like. Then I saw this fair-haired girl, slim,
very pretty, in blue denims, carrying a canvas bag,
looking a little bewildered. I did not hesitate. I
went up to her. 'Are you M?' I asked. And from
that moment there was the happiness of unselfcon-
scious companionship. She was on another visit a
year later when she carried Ambrose in a little
basket to the honeysuckle meadow, where we
buried him.

Then there was the lady whom I had known in
New York when she was twenty-two, a young actress without a care in the world. She had kept in
touch with me, and had now insisted on a reunion.
I awaited apprehensively at the same spot in the

station where I had waited for M. I did not feel the occasion was going to be a success. My one-time girlfriend had enjoyed a successful career as an actress and a playwright, and now lived in an apartment on her own in the Park Avenue area of New York; and no doubt would have different values in regard to domestic comfort. So true.

'I don't think your maid keeps this room very tidy,' she said on arrival at three-room Minack cottage.

I am chronically untidy. No maid could ever keep a room of mine tidy, and of course I haven't got one. I have Joan who comes on a Monday, and she does her best to tidy the untidiness.

'There are not enough hooks on the bathroom door,' was her remark after I had shown her the small bedroom and adjacent bathroom; and when next day I took her out in the car, she said as we crossed Monty's Leap, 'That dip is bad for your car. You ought to fill it in.' Still, she had made the effort to see me, though she regretted it. 'I'll never come to Cornwall again,' she wrote in her thank-you letter. Sad, though, that youthful, carefree relationships die.

I was now away from the station, travelling the road which went past the harbour. On my right there used to be the Jackson warehouse where we sold our tomatoes and lettuces. I would arrive excitedly in OPA 40, the Land-Rover, and ask Fred Galley the foreman what the market was like and, if it was good, he would respond with a wide smile, and if it was bad he would try to be encouraging.

Then on past the Trinity House headquarters on the right, which I used angrily to contact when Tater-du, our unmanned local lighthouse fog signal, blared pointlessly on a clear day. Next I went past Penzance swimming pool, and the promenade which stretched to Newlyn. Now I was nearing home, and I was murmuring to myself silly remarks like, 'I'll be with you in fifteen minutes, Cherry.' On my right was the Queen's Hotel. Here it was that Jeannie used to stay as a child with her family before travelling to Bryher Island in the Scilly Isles. Billy Tunmore was a page boy then, head porter when Jeannie and I frequented the hotel. We went there to use the telephone since we had no wish to have a telephone at the cottage. Thus we used the Queen's as our telephone base. A few chosen people knew of this and they would leave messages, and Billy Tunmore would pass them on when next we called, which could be a week later. All very haphazard.

The Queen's, at the time, had the most beautifully situated bar in Cornwall, overlooking Mount's Bay from where at midday you could watch the *Scillonian* arriving from the Islands. Frank was the barman who one week won a large amount on the football pools, and greeted us with: 'What will you have? Anything you like. Champagne?' He was a friend. Sometimes we would arrive and there were no customers, and Frank would be reading a newspaper. He would be engrossed in his newspaper, wouldn't notice our arrival: 'Sorry, Frank,' I would say, 'to interrupt you . . .' It was in Frank's bar that I once addressed a fellow customer, anxious to draw him into conversation, by asking, 'What do you do?'

'Mind your own bloody business!' was the reply.

I was now passing David Drew's greengrocer's shop near Newlyn Bridge, then up Paul Hill which is steep, then on to the incongruously called hamlet of Sheffield where there is a telephone box which I have often used; and then on to Trevelloe Hill, and to Lamorna Bridge to the turn-off to Lamorna that leads to the welcoming hostelries of the Wink and Lamorna Cove Hotel, and to the then Post Office whence I once had to collect the donkeys, Merlin and Susie, who had escaped from Minack, and were eating the Post Office garden.

At the top of Boleigh Hill I turned left, past a renovated old Cornish cottage, then along the lane potholed by monster tractors and heavy lorries, past the haphazard collection of buildings, past the home of my friends Mary and Mike Nicholls, and Mary's father Bill Trevorrow. They belonged to the beginning of our time at Minack, when a horse pulled the plough, when the milk churns were carried in a cart to the end of the lane every morning, when there was silence in the fields, no transistors blaring from noisy tractors, when no one thought of destroying ancient hedges, when the pace was slow, and village people found contentment in simple things.

There on my right was the sign 'Private Road to Dorminack', and I noticed that the lettering was fading, and I made a mental note that it must be marked up again. Dorminack was always referred to locally as Minack, the 'i' being pronounced as in 'mine'. Hence my reason for the use of the name Minack instead of Dorminack. A few miles along the coast, beautifully placed on the cliffs near Porthcurno is the Minack Theatre, created out of the cliffs by a remarkable woman called Dorothy Cade. It used to be called the Open Air Theatre, signposts advertised it as such; and it is stated as such on the Ordance Survey map. After I had written three of the Minack Chronicles, the management decided to change its name to the Minack Theatre (pronounced Minnack). The Theatre produces memorable productions during the course of the summer. Yet the management has constantly to be on tenterhooks. Is it going to rain tonight? The problem of anyone who has an open-air theatre. Audiences, however, are never put off. The weather is worth risking in order to enjoy a magical evening with the sea lapping the rocks below the stage.

I was now within a minute of home.

'Home! Home!' I heard the echo of Jeannie's voice in my mind, crying out after her first stay in hospital.

The winding lane sloped downwards, blooms of Coverack Glory daffodils on either side, blooms from non-commercial daffodils we had thrown there at random, bright with yellow, resembling a throng lining the streets to cheer the Queen. There were patches of blackthorn, soft white, leafless, first blossoms of spring. The first stalks of the bracken were showing, the first buds of the hawthorn, cushions of gorse, bundles of primroses and wild violets, and, in the distance, the sea.

We had built the lane after we first arrived, for there was no road access to Minack. We paid for it ourselves, and I remember how my mother was with us when the work was completed, and how enraged she was when we saw a neighbouring farmer being the first to use it. Jeannie was on my mother's side, and the two of them wanted to rush out and berate the person concerned . . . and I had to restrain them. 'Don't be so FE,' I said. FE is short for Fire Eating.

But on this occasion I had no reason to feel FE. I was coming home. I was coming back to a place where I felt free, where I didn't have to be on guard. The superficial world would be behind me. I would wake up in the morning with gentle reality around me.

I reached the corner of the lane where the sign stands.

THE DEREK AND JEANNIE TANGYE
MINACK CHRONICLES
NATURE RESERVE
A PLACE FOR SOLITUDE

It is the sign I took to Jeannie two days before she died. In front of it as I pass was a clump of California daffodils. A yard or two away was the gate into Oliver land, the gate which I call Solitude gate because it is by the sign where Merlin and

Susie often hold court, standing there hopefully, favouring those who have brought carrots or biscuits, turning their bottoms on those who haven't.

It is Oliver land that they are in, the twenty acres we bought, and for which we created the Minack Chronicles Nature Trust that will hopefully mean it will be unchanged for ever. Here one is entranced by the sweep of the sea, the curving horizon which begins with the tip of the Lizard, and disappears to the west, Gwennap Head and Land's End. Giant waves on stormy days, weird patterns of currents on still days.

No donkeys to be seen. I passed the sign, and went on down the narrow lane to Monty's Leap, and when I reached it, I was thinking back on the many, many times Jeannie and I had crossed it . . . and of that first time, that midnight, when we first arrived to live at Minack.

Monty was with us. Monty the ginger cat whom I first met as a kitten in Room 205, the Savoy Hotel, Jeannie's office; and who was to convert me from a cat hater:

A full moon was waiting to greet us at Minack, a soft breeze from the sea and the Lizard Light winked every few seconds across Mount's Bay. An owl hooted in the wood, and afar off I heard the wheezing bark, like a hyena, of a vixen. A fishing boat chugged by, a mile offshore, its starboard light bright on the mast. It was very still. The boulders, so massive in the day, had become gossamer in the moonlight, and the cottage, so squat and solid, seemed to be floating in the centuries of its past.

I said to Jeannie: 'Let's see if Monty will come for a walk.'

He came very slowly down the lane, peering suddenly at dangers in the shadows, sitting down and watching us, then softly stepping forward again. His white shirt-front gleamed like a lamp. He sniffed the air, his little nose puzzling the source of the scents of water-weeds, bluebells and the sea. He found a log and clawed it, arching his back. He heard the rustle of a mouse and he became tense, alert to pounce. I felt as I watched him that he was an adventurer prying his private unknown, relishing the prospect of surprise and of the dangers which would be of his own making.

We paused by the little stream, waiting for him to join us and, when he did, he rubbed his head affectionately against my leg, until suddenly he saw the pebbles of the moonlight on the water. He put out a paw as if to touch them.

'I'll pick him up and carry him over.'

But when I bent down to do so he struggled from my grasp – and with the spring of a panther he leapt across and into the shadows beyond.

'Well done!' we cried, 'well done!'

This little stream where it crosses the lane as if it were the moat of Minack, halting the arrival of strangers, greeting us on our returns, acting as a watch on our adventures, was given a name that night.

Monty's Leap.

II

I crossed Monty's Leap and entered my citadel. I felt safe again but I also felt uneasy. How had I behaved? What impression had I made? I did not feel pleased with myself.

The object of my visit was to promote goodwill for my soon-to-be-published book. My task was to mix in the literary scene, making my presence felt. I had forgotten, however, that conversation in such circles is usually anaemic and cliquish, and far removed from the gusto of Minack conversation. Thus my confidence, my over-confidence with which I had set out, was misplaced; and as a result there was a slip-up or two.

The visit began well. I arrived at Claridge's to be welcomed as I got out of the taxi by Barry and Roman, the hall porters; then I went through the revolving door and up the steps to the hall and was greeted again with the warmth of old friends by those at the desk, John Fahr and John Wyvern, Martin and Thomas, then across from the lift came Luigi with outstretched hands, and he took me up to the third floor and to a suite of spacious rooms overlooking Brook Street; and decorating the sitting-room were bouquets of flowers from my publishers, from Ronald Jones the general manager, and from Michael Bentley the manager with a note attached: 'Welcome to your London home.' Claridge's with its elegant quietness is indeed a hotel which makes you feel at home.

When I first arrived in London after leaving Harrow, I was glad to have a job as a junior clerk with Unilever, in their offices near Blackfriars Bridge. I knew only one girl in London at the time, but she happened to be a débutante; and in those days the débutante season during the summer was one long list of balls and elaborate dinner parties beforehand. As a result of my acquaintance with this girl and her family, I began to be invited to an increasing number of balls and dinner parties, and by so doing I gradually became an accepted deb's delight. Then came the time when I resigned from Unilever because I was fed up with office work, and wanted to become a writer. Any doubts as to whether I had acted stupidly in resigning were removed when I visited a phrenologist who had a consulting room in one of the buildings around Ludgate Circus; 'You're destined,' I was told, 'to be a journalist or an interior decorator.'

I was now out of a job, writing articles which were not accepted but . . . I was a deb's delight. I survived that summer by being, one might say, a professional deb's delight, for which there were perks, and a ball at Claridge's was one of the first to provide me with such perks. Tails and white tie was the uniform of a deb's delight, and the tails had big pockets, and at the end of a ball I would go to the buffet, choose the delicacies I liked, and put them in the pockets. Thus I was assured that the next day's larder was full. Just as well: I was living on £3 a week which my father gave me.

I became a journalist as the phrenologist of Ludgate Circus told me I should, and I went to Manchester for a couple of years, then came back to London, and soon Claridge's was again on the fringe of my life. I had fallen in love with a movie star, a sloe-eyed, slim dark girl called Sylvia Sidney. Was it *City Streets* or *Street Scene* I first saw her in? I cannot remember. But what I do remember was that I saw in an evening newspaper that she had arrived in London and was staying at Claridge's. This was an opportunity not to be missed, so I asked my editor innocently, not telling him of my personal interest, whether I could interview her. He agreed.

I arrived at Claridge's, gave my name and that of my newspaper at the enquiry desk and was ushered up to Sylvia Sidney's suite on the fourth floor. I recall nothing of the interview except that I was bewitched. There was this darling creature whom I had loved from a cinema seat, sitting within a few feet of me. Even a closer relationship was soon to develop. At the end of the interview I timidly asked if I could show her the sights of London by night . . . and she accepted.

I was now faced with a practical problem. I had no car. I could not possibly afford a hired car, and in any case every penny I possessed was allocated to the dinner in a Soho restaurant which I had suggested, Soho being an area which she particularly wanted to visit. What was I to do?

It was now that I had a brilliant idea. One of my fellow deb's delights had a sister who was married to a senior member of MI5. A few weeks previously my friend had given my name to his sister and her husband, saying that I was a journalist whom he liked. Not long after I was contacted by the husband, and after outlining what he wanted me to do, he said that if he could help me at any time in the future he would be happy to do so. The mission he asked me to do was to make certain interviews, under the guise of being a journalist, about the background behaviour of an officer in a Scottish regiment called Baillie Stewart; and the alleged connections this officer had with the German Secret Service.

I agreed to follow his instructions, but I couldn't wait for him to fulfil his promise to help me in the future. He could help me *now*. I had this beautiful girl willing to see London at night with me . . . and this man had a car.

'Could you lend me your car tonight?' I asked boldly.

'Certainly,' he replied charmingly, then added, 'I'm afraid it will be my second car. I need the other myself.'

'Doesn't matter at all,' I said eagerly.

'All right, here are the keys. It is outside in the drive.'

I went outside, and found a Baby Austin.

A Baby Austin was the vogue car of the time but it was so small that one compared it with a postage stamp on a large envelope. It was certainly not a car that the hall porters would expect to arrive at Claridge's, nor would it be considered suitable to drive a world-famous film star around the streets of London at night. But the evening travels took place, dinner at Quo Vadis in Frith Street, a tour of London streets, ending up on the Embankment gazing at Battersea Power Station, the first floodlit building in London. Sylvia Sidney said that it had been a memorable evening, and I was grateful to her for the compliment. As for myself it had been also a memorable evening ... I had been so over-whelmed by the presence at my side of my dream girl that for most of the time I had been tongue-tied.

There were other connections with Claridge's which made me nostalgic. The tycoon whose news-paper I then worked for was also involved in the film industry, and the occasion arose when he thought he might be able to amalgamate with Twen-tieth Century Fox whose president at the time was Joe Schenk. I was deputed to go to Claridge's and interview this Hollywood mogul, and to write a two-part series of his life. 'Be nice,' warned the editor. As it was I was captivated by the sheer ruthlessness of Joe Schenk's story, and by just re-porting his words, the aim was achieved. There was no cause for me to express a personal opinion.

Then there was another American mogul whom

I was sent to interview ... William Randolph Hearst. He was at Claridge's with his long-established mistress, the movie star Marion Davies. He was a large man with a bulky tummy so that his jacket and shirt lay in folds when he sat down in a chair which was too small for him. I interviewed him for an hour, fascinated I have to admit, that I was talking with one of the most powerful people in the United States. At last the interview was over, and I left the suite, and began walking down the corridor to the lift. I was about to reach it when I heard someone calling me. It was Marion Davies. She was tripping hastily down the corridor. 'Do me a favour,' I heard her say, 'write something about me. *He* ...' and she jerked her thumb over her shoulder '... is getting all the publicity this trip!'

I had a significant experience at Claridge's during the early part of the Hitler war before the United States joined in the conflict and when the US administration was probing as to whether Britain, standing alone, truly had the full backing of those in power, or close to power. All sorts of rumours had been running about concerning certain figures in the Westminster political world who would be prepared to come to terms with Hitler. The American administration therefore sent investigators, some of them with no normal contact with the US Government, to Britain to see what they could find out.

One of these men was Paul Smith, editor of the *San Francisco Chronicle*, whom I had known, and in whose newspaper I had written, when I was on my world tour in the year before war broke out. He was staying at Claridge's, and my boss in MI5, which I had now joined, told me to go and see him. It was a pleasant April day, I remember, so pleasant that after he poured me a drink we took our drinks out to the balcony overlooking Brook Street. We chatted, then he said something which startled me.

'I went to see Lloyd George this morning,' he said, 'and I found him terribly depressed . . . and I came away saying to myself that this man was waiting to be the English Pétain.'

This news was on Churchill's desk the next morning.

For me, my most happy nostalgic memory of Claridge's was when Jeannie hosted the lunch for Roy Plomley and his producer Derek Drescher before I was the castaway on *Desert Island Discs*. Roy Plomley, the originator of the programme, will always remain the superior of any subsequent presenter. He was so gentle, intuitive, and with his melodious voice he made listeners feel so comfortable, as if Roy Plomley and his castaway were sitting with them in their own homes. I was surprised how nervous he was. When I was there, answering his questions in a tiny studio, he kept dropping the discs on to the floor. It helped me not to feel so nervous myself. Jeannie and I had spent six months preparing for the programme, choosing discs, discarding them, choosing them again . . . but I have spent the time since that day thinking of all the

music I would like to have chosen but didn't. Roy
Plomley in his book *Plomley's Pick* chose me as
one of his fifty most favourite castaways.

It was at Claridge's that Jeannie was instrumen-
tal in launching Christian Dior into the English
fashion scene, Dior who revolutionized the way
women were to dress after the austerity of the war
years. Here is how Jeannie did it, a classic example
of how a top-class publicity person operates. I
quote from her book, *Meet Me at the Savoy*:

I remember the time when the 'New Look' was a
front-page story, although the longer skirts had
not yet crossed the Channel. Looking through Claridge's house list I saw the name 'Dior' with initial
'C'. I did not wait to telephone, but called a taxi
and rushed round to Brook Street. 'Yes,' said a
receptionist with a shrug of the shoulders. 'I believe it is Monsieur Christian Dior, but he is leaving for France almost immediately.'

I telephoned Dior's apartment. 'There will soon
be a very important fashion writer to see him in
the front hall. Would he grant her five minutes on
the way out?' The answer was yes, and so I rang
Anne Edwards of the *Daily Express*, and within
twenty minutes she was at Claridge's, accompanied
by Robb the fashion artist. The next day appeared
the exclusive interview in the *Daily Express* with
Robb's sketch called the 'New Look'. That is how
the description the 'New Look' became a part for
ever of fashion language.

Here it was at Claridge's that Jeannie used to be

chased goodhumouredly around the tables by Mi-
landra, the charming restaurant manager, when she
arrived to find out what celebrities might be lunch-
ing there (sexual harassment it would be called
today . . . Jeannie called it fun).

Here it was that Jeannie caused a diplomatic
incident. Sumner Welles, Under Secretary at the
US State Department, was coming to London on
behalf of President Roosevelt on a delicate mission
to discover how the United States could help Britain in the early part of the Hitler war before the
United States was involved.

A suite was booked for him at Claridge's, and
Jeannie, unwisely, thought this was a publicity opportunity, and she arranged for a press photographer to take a picture of the suite. Unfortunately
the photographer asked her to appear herself in the
photograph . . . and next day it appeared in a national newspaper with a very pretty Jeannie standing there as if she was included in the suite. The
booking was cancelled, and Sumner Welles went
elsewhere. Jeannie nearly lost her job.

Look through the index of her book, and one
catches a glimpse of Jeannie's world before she
came to Minack: American mission, Prince Bern-
hard, Mr and Mrs Churchill, Election Night, end
of war, King of Greece, Harry Hopkins, Alexander
Korda, General Montgomery, Merle Oberon,
Mrs Roosevelt, Russian Military Mission, Royal
Wedding Guests, Barbara Stanwyck, Queen
Wilhelmina, Duke of Windsor, King Peter of Yugo-
slavia . . .

Of all the above, General Montgomery had the most influence on our lives. On the day he had arrived at Claridge's, a ginger kitten, the colour of autumn bracken, was found by me in Jeannie's Savoy office, Room 205, with Jeannie's secretary teasing it with a typewriter ribbon. The kitten which was to be called Monty. The kitten which was to change me from a cat hater to a cat convert. The kitten who was to become *A Cat in the Window*. The kitten who earned its name after General Montgomery, victor of El Alamein.

Now here I was at Claridge's alone, and about to go to a literary dinner. I had to wear a dinner suit. My dinner suit had hung for a long time unused in a cupboard in what I call the confusion room. It fitted me, which was one obstacle overcome. I had bought a new evening shirt but there was the question of the tie. I had always used a loose tie, a tie that I could tie myself. An artificial tie fixed easily by a clip was, I was always led to believe, socially incorrect. I was involved in tie snobbism.

After a bath, after putting on my shirt, the time came for me to tie the tie; and I had forgotten how to do it. I fiddled with it, I twisted it, I pulled it, I screamed at it, but there was no co-operation from the tie. Panic. I pressed a button for help, and a valet quickly arrived.

'Sir,' he said, after fumbling with the tie for a few moments, 'I think a fixed tie would be more suitable. We always have spares and I will fetch one.'

All was well, and I set out for the literary dinner wearing a Claridge's tie.

I arrived early. There was a series of ante-rooms, sparsely filled, and I walked through them until I came to the final one where a small group was gathered, an air of distinction about them. I was standing there at a loss when out of the group stepped a charming lady towards me, who without a moment's hesitation greeted me by saying: 'I must introduce you to one of your greatest fans.' This was flattery beyond the realms of fantasy; and I was to learn later that she had been a literary editor of distinction.

It was now that I made a slip-up. The lady's flattery had disarmed me. My vanity was tickled that I was considered so worthy of her attention, of the group's attention. I was caught off balance. I was not quick enough to realize that, as I was the first guest to arrive, there was nothing else for anyone to do but to greet me. So I stood there, foolish enough to believe that the greeting had the same sincerity as that of anyone being greeted at Minack.

I started to talk about Cornwall, about Minack, thinking that the fan, the lady, and the others in the group might be interested in a world so different to their own. As I gabbled on, however, I observed a pained look coming over their faces and I was to realize in retrospect that I was talking a language which they did not understand. The conversation lasted only a few minutes but there was time for me to make a final blunder.

'How do people find you?' one of the group asked faintheartedly.

'That's the point,' I replied, 'I'm so difficult to find, the cottage so remote, that only those who really *want* to come arrive, and as a result I know they are genuine readers, and they are of all ages, from all spheres, and often we become friends and keep in touch.'

There was a chilly silence. Then I blundered on.

'You see,' I said, 'I've always felt that the kind of book I like to read is one which reaches the minds of people so that the reader feels involved.'

I had lost my small audience. They were moving away.

Next came a luncheon my publishers gave me.

Those in publishing have a workload that members of the public have no knowledge of. They see a book in a bookshop, and that's that. However, the book they see has been on a long journey.

The author gives birth to the idea for the book, then picks up a blank piece of paper and writes Chapter One. Then follows months of struggle, periods of writer's block, elation when the mind runs free, gloom again when on reading what he has written he doesn't like it, and the wastepaper basket receives another contribution.

The publisher receives the manuscript along with scores of other manuscripts, and has the perilous task of deciding which to accept, always aware of the resulting heartbreak caused by the return of the manuscripts unwanted. The accepted manuscript now becomes like a unit in a factory. There is the costing, the editing, the designing of the jacket, the printing, the sales and promotion plans, the date of publication, and finally the distribution to the shops. Each book is very personal to the author, and the publisher has the awesome task of dealing with many such personal books.

I made no obvious blunder at the lunch. Everyone was so kind and much trouble had been taken to make me welcome. Yet I found myself feeling inhibited. I decided it would be best not to talk about Minack. It was too delicate a story. I could not be sure, after my experience at the literary dinner, that everyone there would understand the subtleties; and so I felt it would be wiser to be on safe ground, and talk about my life in MI5.

Roger Hollis was again in the news at the time . . . Roger Hollis, once head of MI5, had been systematically accused by sections of the media of being a Soviet agent. I had been closely associated with him during my ten years at MI5, as I had also been with Blunt and Philby. Maclean and Burgess, on the other hand, I knew in a more remote capacity.

Once, for instance, I sent Blunt a memo warning him that I had a contact who was suspicious of Burgess. How Blunt and Burgess must have laughed! The contact was an American who had lunched with Burgess and one of Burgess's friends, while the fourth member of the party was an official in the Swiss Government. My contact considered the intense questioning of the official by Burgess to be most peculiar. There was a curious aftermath to this story. My contact was later refused a permit to stay in this country. I have often wondered . . . did Blunt, still in a position of influence, trace through Burgess the source of my memo, and use his influence to cancel the permit?

Blunt made use of me from time to time on behalf of his KGB masters. He would ask me to make inquiries about individuals which I took for granted were legitimate MI5 inquiries. I had no cause to be suspicious of him. True, he did not impress me. He had no warmth. I was never relaxed in the company of Blunt.

He also belonged to a clique in the MI5 office, and I have always felt from my schooldays antagonistic to those who belong to a clique. He, Burgess and Philby belonged to a clique which included Lord Victor Rothschild. Rothschild had a brilliant war record as a scientist and anti-sabotage expert. He was responsible for introducing Blunt into MI5, and he also gave financial support to his friend Burgess.

Roger Hollis did not belong to this clique. I first came into contact with him when I had been asked to prepare a monthly report on the work of every section of MI5 which would then be circulated among the sections. An imaginative idea to keep everyone informed as to what was happening to MI5. When I went to see Hollis, however, to inquire into the activities of his section, he was most uncooperative. 'Supposing,' he said, 'this newssheet of yours got into the wrong hands? It would be disastrous.' And of course it *did* get into the wrong hands. My monthly report, via Blunt, was passed to the KGB. Thus I was innocently responsible for providing Blunt with a coup.

I never met Maclean, but four years after the Hitler war ended, an agent of mine told me he had been at the famous Gargoyle nightclub the night before with Maclean; and Maclean had got drunk and began blurting out reasons for his pro-Soviet sympathies. My agent had been made particularly suspicious by one remark Maclean had made, and for this reason he had come to see me. He suggested that MI5 should pay his expenses for further meetings with Maclean; and he proposed the sum of £50, but authority for the money to be paid was not given.

As for Hollis, I did not think him very bright, and I have always been puzzled as to why he was appointed Head of MI5 in the first place. He made several errors of judgement during his time at MI5 but they were mistakes born of lack of imagination. He was no spy, but some of his mistakes made him appear to be a spy, thus fuelling those in the media who were looking for sensations.

The media, meanwhile, were acting as unknowing agents of the KGB, spreading misinformation not only about Hollis but about others such as my friend Guy Liddell, one-time head of my department. The KGB in Moscow relished the confusion that was being caused. 'They are laughing their heads off,' said Gordievsky, Head of the KGB Centre in London until he defected.

Exposure of the Cambridge spies has now been completed with the Cairncross confession. Of the five, Philby was the most ruthless. After meeting him for the first time I returned to Jeannie and

26

told her I had been in conference with a man I had immediately distrusted. No logical reason for such a feeling. The exposure of the spies may have been completed but there is still one mystery to be solved.

In 1941 I was told by an officer of MI5 for whom I had great respect that the KGB were recruiting university undergraduates, and had been doing so for some while. 'The Russians,' he said, 'are very patient. They will recruit a young man with communist views, tell him to dissociate himself from the Party, watch him, and keep him on ice for years. Then one day they will come to him and say: "Now we want you to do this . . ."'

If this knowledge existed in MI5, how can one explain the success of the Cambridge spies?

One could believe there was a sinister reason, that they were protected by someone in MI5. I am certain that this could not have been possible for any length of time. More likely it was due to stupidity and lack of imagination, and the supreme belief that members of the upper class could not possibly be Communists, let alone betray their country. Nor was there any realism towards the Soviet threat. During the war there was one officer, one assistant and a secretary in charge of watching the whole KGB apparatus. No wonder Blunt, Burgess, Philby and Maclean could wander around London, meeting their case officers without fear of detection.

Next I went to a lunch the Savoy Directors were giving for ex-Press Officers of the Savoy Group, to which I was invited to represent Jeannie. It was held in the River Room; and it was in the River Room that I first saw Jeannie, and where we had our first dinner together. The windows were boarded up then, no glimpse of the London river; bombs falling, anti-aircraft guns blazing, were our companions in those days.

Now I was there again: there were the same pillars, the same floor, and all those years in between. I remembered the moment when, as I toyed with roast duck and red wine sauce, garnished with grapes, I asked Jeannie for her full name; and she replied that it was Jean Everald Nicol. I remembered how I gasped, and how I said: 'Good heavens, you're the girl I'm going to marry!' and this because I had had my hand read on a Japanese boat sailing from Sydney to Hong Kong, and the palmist, an engineer, who read my hand had told me just that: 'She'll be darker and smaller than yourself, and her initials will be J. E.'

I found my diary of that period a couple of weeks ago, and on looking through it I found the page which recorded the prophecy. There it was in my handwriting, written within an hour or two of it being told me. I touched the page; and I was stabbed by the memory of the magical years since I first touched it. Here is what I wrote:

9 April 1939.
For the first time in my life I've had my fortune told. Parkinson who had studied with Cheiro said that my health would always be good, that I'll be

successful though I'll have to fight hard and sometimes be right down, and that the next two years
are going to be very difficult, that 1941 is going to
bring me one success greater than I've ever had
[*Time Was Mine* was published then], that my
marrying year is 1943 or 4, that in the next twelve
months a girl with the initial J. or J. E. is going to
be very important, and that my wife would be
smaller than I, and dark.

I had not been to the Savoy since Jeannie died,
and when I entered Room 205, her office on the
first floor, there were echoes in my mind . . . laughter, dramas, the sparkling fun of Jeannie, her long
dark hair, slim exquisite figure, her ability to en-
chant anyone who came to see her, operating in a
man's world without any need for Equal Opportunity laws to make her job secure, relying on her
femininity, her common sense, her expertise, her
sex appeal. There I was in Room 205 again, remembering:

'Jeannie, I have to go off to the Palace for a dress
rehearsal, would you look after Simon for me?'
    The spaniel looked at Jeannie.
    'Yes, of course,' she said.
    David Milford Haven, Best Man at the Queen's
wedding to Prince Philip, was grateful.
    'I'll be back as soon as I can.'

'Danny,' said Jeannie to Danny Kaye, 'Gertie is
feeling lonely. She's so famous that no one dares
to ask her out.'

Gertie being Gertie Lawrence who had just opened in the play *September Tide* by Daphne du Maurier.

Danny picked up the phone on Jeannie's desk.

'Gee,' he said, 'will you be my girl tonight? Princess Margaret is giving a party.'

Jeannie to James Mason.

'You can't, James, bring your cats to stay at the Savoy!'

'But, Jeannie, I have to, there is nowhere else for them to go; Jeannie, you of all people should understand!'

'All right, but don't tell anyone . . . such a good story but I can't tell anyone either.'

My mother on the day we became engaged.

'How are you celebrating?' she asked.

'We're having a bottle of champagne,' Jeannie replied.

'A *whole* bottle?' asked my mother.

'Oh yes,' said Jeannie gaily, 'this is the second bottle!'

A. P. Herbert sitting on the office sofa, pen and paper in hand, trying to write a speech he expected to make in the House of Commons that afternoon.

'I give up,' he said despairingly, 'Mr Somerset will help me. Come with me, Jeannie.'

Mr Somerset, doyen of Heppell's the chemist in the Strand, who catered for many famous people with hangovers.

'What's this?' I said to Lois, Jeannie's secretary,

looking down at the object on the green carpet of
the office. 'What on earth is this kitten doing here?'
I had seen ambassadors, film stars, cabinet minis-
ters, famous international journalists, politicians
of all parties, in Jeannie's office but I had never
before met a cat.

'Come on,' I said, 'come on, Lois, tell me what
it is all about?' But Lois, the perfect secretary,
went on playing as if she hadn't heard me. 'Lois,'
I went on, 'you're hiding something from me.
Where's Jeannie? What's she been up to? Both of
you know I dislike cats and if . . .'

John Steinbeck coming shyly into Room 205,
saying to Jeannie: 'I want to thank you for making
everything so comfortable for me,' then adding
gently, 'I suppose you wouldn't like to have a drink
with me.'

Carroll Gibbons, legendary band leader of the
Savoy Orpheans, saying: 'You are so beautiful,
honey, so beautiful.' And whenever Jeannie appeared in the restaurant at night Carroll would
change whatever music the band was playing to
'Jeannie With the Light Brown Hair', that lovely
Stephen Foster song . . . and people at their tables
would look to see who deserved this special switch
of Carroll's music.

I was remembering, too, some of those who
helped to create the fun Jeannie had at the Savoy.
Fred Snow of the inquiry desk; head porters like
Hansen and Tollardo; Joe Gilmore of the American
Bar; Polosi and Sava of the Grill; the famous

mercurial Luigi Donzelli of the Grill, later of
Claridge's; the suave, elegant Santarelli of the
Restaurant; Aldo of the Grill; Townsend and
Burke of the Cloakroom; Chamberlain, head porter
of the Embankment Entrance, and his colleagues;
and the great chefs Latry and Trompetto . . . there
was this wonderful Savoy comradeship which inspired people to work together. Jeannie was loved
by them, and members of the staff would come to
her when they had a special problem. She never let
them down. The heroes of her three hotel novels
were the staff of a great London hotel; and the
third novel, her last, centres around the reunion,
the happy reunion, of past members of such a
London hotel.

Here I was at a real-life reunion, and I sat at the
table of Sir Hugh Wontner, Chairman of the Savoy
Group for many years. During his time the Group
had to fight off several potential takeovers from
companies whose object was to cash in on the
Savoy Group's untarnished reputation throughout
the world.

These financial predators found, to their chagrin,
a stumbling block in the person of Sir Hugh. He
was not in the City sense a conventional chairman.
He was immune to financial gains. He was immune
to the mud which was sometimes thrown at him.
The driving force of his life has been to keep the
Savoy Group free from opportunists. He has integrity. He was determined that the hotels would continue to maintain the highest hotel standards in the
world.

We were given a booklet at the lunch:

From the days when Mr Richard D'Oyly Carte introduced all sorts of innovations into his theatre [the Savoy Theatre] and later into his hotel next door, the Savoy has always been a pioneer in many ways. Among them was the comparatively new idea of marketing.

The Savoy began this first in New York around 1927 but the Press Office, later to have Public Relations added to it, began even earlier.

The gloomy period of the First World War had ended, and the Savoy invented the idea of 'Brighter Britain'. This eventually turned into the 'Come to Britain' movement, then into the British Travel Association, and finally into the present British Tourist Authority.

Then came the final paragraph which touched me very much.

Presiding over the Press Office at that time was a man of extraordinary influence. If he wanted something to be made public (or the reverse) he knew how to do it. His name was Richmond Temple.

Since then, the Savoy Press Office has been a centre of activity for the Company, and the background of many careers in Public Relations. One of the most notable has been Jean Nicol Tangye (Mrs Derek Tangye), the author of *Meet Me at the Savoy*, which went into more than seventeen editions.

How proud I was to have represented Jeannie.

III

I had come home, leaving behind the unsettling mood which led Jeannie and me to come to Minack. The pace had changed. Concorde speed instead of Constellation. Speed, speed, no time to contemplate. Decisions made for the effect, not for the substance. Image makers in control.

> The glamour and the hospitality act as a narcotic, doping the finer instincts of living, and in the grey hours of early morning you lie awake painfully aware that you live in a flashy world where truth and integrity for the most part are despised, where slickness reigns supreme.
>
> We found the pace too fast and the material rewards poor substitutes for the peace of mind which was sacrificed. The world of politics, journalism and entertainment in which we moved requires a ruthless zest for professional survival if you are to do so, and this neither of us now possessed.

I had come home to continue with one aim: to preserve Minack unspoilt for posterity, preserve it for those who seek solitude, for those who wish to unwind, viewing the jagged world and their own lives in perspective. Not just for those who come here, but a place for faraway people to travel to in their minds. Minack will never have coachloads of visitors. Minack is secret. Minack is for the individual, not for the masses. Minack is full of small pleasures, not strident ones.

It is easy to talk about an aim like this, but practical problems proliferate. What happens if I am run over by a bus? Whom can I rely upon to carry on the aim? Those who may be prepared to do so today may have changed their ideas when the time comes. A sensitive guardian is needed, someone who is imbued with the story of the Minack Chronicles, and a practical one who can deal with inevitable complications.

Sometimes I look through my letter files to seek encouragement. They do not fail me. They are my anchors. Here is one:

My spirit was totally given up to Minack. I was completely lost in its breathtaking beauty. I was very forcibly struck by a glorious, incredible, unchallengeable truth, the truth called Destiny. My dictionary defines Destiny as a 'state pre-determined – an inevitable necessity'. How true is that last statement – an inevitable necessity. For it was a *necessity* that you and Jeannie should live at Minack. A *necessity* because you have given hope to countless thousands of people, the most marvellous gift anyone can bestow.

Everything that has happened since that day you saw the cottage from the Carn, saw your future, saw your 'figures moving about our daily tasks, a thousand, thousand figures criss-crossing the untamed land, dissolving into each other, leaving a mist of excitement of our times to come' – everything which has happened since you wrote those lines *had* to happen. How that passage from *A Gull on the Roof* moves me. Destiny being fulfilled is an awe-inspiring thought. Minack is forever the home of you and Jeannie, the home of Monty, of Lama, of Oliver, of Ambrose, of Cherry, of Penny and Fred, of Boris the drake, of Hubert and his gull successors, of Merlin and Susie.

We rented the two-room cottage and the twenty acres of derelict land around it for £25 a year from an old Cornish family when we first came. Then we set about opening up the land, and creating small meadows which stretched down to the sea of Mount's Bay and resembled a vineyard. Here we grew our daffodils and early potatoes until horticultural progress caught up with us, and it was no longer profitable to work them. Now the daffodils blossom unpicked, peering through the undergrowth which has taken over the meadows that we once had taken such care and hard work to open up. Then, a few years ago, in curious circumstances, we were able to buy twenty acres on the other side of the valley, not to produce anything on it, but to conserve it. We called it Oliver land because it was in the corner of the large field where the donkeys graze, and where we first saw Oliver the black cat, who was to become the hero of *When the Winds Blow*. This is the land protected by the

Minack Chronicles Nature Trust, the land which I have stated in my will shall never be sold, the land I was worried about should I be run over by a bus, along with the worry as to how to link Minack cottage and the rented land with the Trust land. Minack cottage has been listed Grade II by the Department of the Environment English Heritage division because of the Chronicles. It has, therefore, an umbrella of official protection. Oliver land does not have such protection.

A week had passed since my return. I had calmed down, unwinding into the routine of Minack life. Cherry had been visited daily by Joan Johnson. Joan has been coming to Minack every Monday for a long time, to help first Jeannie, then me.

Joan's husband Ron is the driver of a milk lorry and his hours of work require him to leave home at five in the morning. Joan's day starts at that hour as well: housework, taking Cindy her dog for a walk, feeding her four cats before making the mile walk to Minack, arriving at about nine. She would have a carrier bag with her, and out of it she would produce a carton of milk, bread and a tin of cat food for Cherry; and when at the end of the day I would offer to pay for it, she would refuse any money. I would press her and she would continue to refuse.

She first heard of Jeannie and me when she read *A Gull on the Roof* during her office luncheon hour in London where she was a secretary. In due course she and Ron decided to leave London and make a new life in the West Country; and eventually they came to Penzance. She came to work for us first as a daffodil picker, and then she began to help Jeannie in the cottage, and they became friends, and Jeannie said to me: 'Joan is one of those rare people whom you can trust absolutely.' Jeannie referred in that remark not just to the help she did around the cottage, but also to her discretion.

Joan loves Cherry. She would arrive after her mile-long walk, and forthwith take charge of the welfare of Cherry as if I was not competent to do so. She would proceed to prise open a tin of cat food, for instance, and I would call out: 'Don't do that. I opened a tin last night!' Joan would ignore me. Then, after I had already given Cherry a bowl of fresh milk, Joan would proceed to give her another ... warmed. 'Cherry likes it warm, don't you, Cherry,' Joan would say.

These scenes reminded me of the long-ago days when I hated cats. The days when I watched people fawning on cats, despising them for doing so. Cats, in my view, were vermin, insensitive vermin, and those who appeared to love them to the point of imbecility were in fact imbeciles. I have long ago dispensed with my brutish cat attitude, but there is always lurking in the back of my mind a distaste for anyone who gushes senselessly at a cat.

So I would banter Joan for her pandering to Cherry as she dolloped out a second helping.

'She's already had a plate of meat chunks and licked it clean,' I would say, 'so she doesn't want any more.'

Undeterred Joan would refill the plate.

'It will be wasted!' I would say crossly.

Joan would then call out for Cherry, holding the plate in her hand; and if she wasn't in the room, Joan would go out into the porch, and if she wasn't in the porch, Joan would go outside, all the time calling 'Cherry!' I would sit waiting for her return, waiting to say, 'I told you so!' But I would never have the chance to say, 'I told you so!' Cherry would always let me down. Joan would return in triumph with the plate empty. 'You win, Joan,' I would say humbly.

Cherry, who came to Minack uninvited and was found by Jeannie one foggy morning beneath the cherry tree, has remained very small as if she were a still growing kitten. She was already spayed when she arrived, about six months old said the vet, and for ever it will remain a mystery whence she came. We tried hard enough in our area to find out, but there was never a clue. Somebody must have loved her, for why otherwise should she have been spayed? Jeannie and I often thought of the person concerned, and the agonizing search for the lost little black cat. Some have suggested that she may have been dumped, but surely anyone who knew Jeannie or had read about her dottiness for cats would have arrived at the door, Cherry in a basket, begging Jeannie to take her because she no longer could be kept in her original home? Jeannie would have yielded, of that I am sure, backed up by a reluctant me. For I would be thinking of Ambrose's reaction, Ambrose the cat king of Minack. Or had Cherry stowed away in a car or a van? Cats have a foolish knack of doing such things ... and so Cherry may have come from far, far away. We also remembered the remark of Beverley Nichols, the great cat lover, the creator in one of his cat books of F and non F as a way of describing people. He often came to Minack, and he once said that when he died he would return to earth in the spirit of a cat. We both had a great affection for Beverley but not sufficient to have him wandering around Minack as a cat. He had died a month before Cherry's arrival.

Cherry is all black except for her apricot-coloured shirt-front and underpants, she has a smudge of white on her back right paw. The front left paw is off-white with a black ribbon through the centre. She has no miaow, just a squeak; and the thought that she might find herself in a dilemma without an alarm bell to attract our attention has always been a worry. Her way of showing affection is to look at us with appealing eyes, then quickly open and shut her little mouth. She purrs, of course, a vibrant purr, but otherwise she is mute.

As time went by after her arrival we noticed that the colour of her coat began to change when spring came. The head, shoulders and little legs remained black, jet black ... but the rest of her body developed a rusty colour. It was her summer coat, we used to say, and, true enough, when winter came, black began to take over again. It was strange, however, to look at her summer coat. Outsiders said the same. The point was that the coat seemed to have taken on the colours, the orange colours, of

Monty and Ambrose. Thus Cherry was a kind of representative of the cats of Minack.

I remained, however, apprehensive of her presence because of Ambrose. Ambrose hated her during those first months, and there were clashes, spits and growls, and chases . . . Ambrose chased her whenever he caught her outside; and indoors, although there was an armed neutrality, Cherry was wise enough to keep to her own room, the spare room, and we kept open the bathroom window through which she could skip in and out unobserved.

I found the stress disturbing, and one day I announced to Jeannie that I could not agree to this guerrilla warfare continuing for the rest of Ambrose's life.

'It's just not fair,' I said.

'So what are you proposing to do?'

'I'm going to give Cherry an examination to pass.'

'And what kind of examination?'

'I'm going to set her a series of tests to pass, which I will call her C-Levels.'

'C for cat?'

'Yes.'

'And what are these C-Levels?'

'There are nine of them, and here is the list:

1. She must not catch birds.
2. She must be house clean.
3. She must not show interest in food on the dining-room table.

4. No rotovating of the carpet with claws.
5. No digging-up of plants in the garden.
6. Must not be too friendly with strangers.
7. Must never wander far.
8. No bringing into the cottage of live mice or rabbits.
9. She must not cause us anxiety at night by hiding when she is called.

After reading them out I said to Jeannie that we should judge the result on the anniversary of her coming to Minack, which would be nine months away. Of course I had no wish for Cherry to fail. I was teasing Jeannie. I was teasing myself. It was a way of showing that I was not neglecting Ambrose, not neglecting the love he had shown us over the years.

And Cherry did not fail. Cherry passed all nine C-Levels, and we celebrated . . . Jeannie and I with a bottle of Moët Chandon, Cherry with a plate of fresh crab, Ambrose with a plate of his favourite coley. From then on Ambrose tolerated Cherry. He was the king, she the princess; and then Ambrose died and Cherry became the queen.

It was this spring that I thought I had lost Cherry. She had never been one to lie regularly on my bed. She liked to chop and change her sleeping venues. Sometimes it was in a cupboard of the spare room or curled on the heap of clothes I often left on the bed, or on the far corner of the table-like shelf which tops the cupboard, and where there are a pile of Bertha jerseys (Bertha is a friend of many years who knits jerseys for me) on which she likes to curl. There are other hideouts, and sometimes she would be so eccentric as to settle among the books of the bookshelf which stands high in front of my Regency desk.

On the night that began the nightmare, when I thought I was going to lose her, she had chosen to sleep at the bottom of my bed. She had not been on the bed for several weeks, and I felt flattered that she had decided to do so; and I fell asleep quietly content that she was there.

Around midnight I was awoken by a commotion at the bottom of the bed. I could not believe what was happening for a moment, then I realized that Cherry was having convulsions, and was flinging herself about, out of control. I put out my hand to hold her, and I had to use all my strength to do so; and as I was trying to hold her, the question as to what I should do was racing through my mind.

I had to get hold of a vet, would have to wake him up ... but where were my spectacles? How could I find his number without spectacles? I was holding her but only just, and I had to press hard to keep her still even for a few seconds, and I didn't know whether I was doing right by holding her so firmly. By luck I felt the spectacles underneath the eiderdown where I had left them after reading a book, and I found the torch below on the floor ... but now I had to have the telephone directory and the radio telephone, and both were just out of reach. I was in despair. Cherry still struggling, me trying to hold her, no nearer getting help. Then, driven by this desperation, I made a lunge for the chest of drawers where stood the telephone and the directory, and somehow picked them up and dumped them beside me. Cherry had gone suddenly quiet, and that upset me. Had she died? I found the number, dialled it, and a sleepy voice replied. I explained what had happened, and as I did so, Cherry gave a lurch. That was a relief. I did not quite know what I expected from the vet but I was content with his advice. It was the only advice I could follow. 'Keep her quiet, but if she has another attack within half an hour ring me again.'

In the morning Cherry was still on the bed, apparently dazed since she did not respond to anything I did. Then the vet came out, looked very serious, shaking his head, and I sensed that he did not think there was much hope for her. He gave her an injection. Then he said:

'She's suffering from an acute form of poisoning ... the next forty-eight hours will be the critical time.'

That evening as I sat on the sofa I heard a thump in the bedroom where Cherry had lain on the bed all day, which was followed by Cherry swaying and stumbling towards the spare room ... the spare room which was her headquarters when Ambrose was king. I followed her, and found she had pushed through a gap in the cupboard and had settled on a jersey at floor level. She was panting, and her eyes had a film over them, and were revolving. It was at that moment I was certain I was going to lose her.

I slept on the floor that night and the next, with a rug as a mattress, and close enough to be able to stroke her. The vet came out, giving her injections while I tried to tempt her with any delicacy I could think of. No luck. She would not touch anything . . . then one wonderful moment on the third day, I dipped a finger in a saucer of milk, offered it her, and a tongue appeared and licked it. For the first time in three days I sensed she was going to recover.

What was the poison which caused all the trouble? I was not able to trace it. Nor could the vet give any help. We could only speculate.

During the late afternoon prior to her midnight convulsions, she had come with me into the bulb field above the cottage where I was picking a basket of the daffodils called Joseph Macleod, named after a BBC wartime announcer of that name.

A Dutchman bred this daffodil during the Hitler war. One evening he had the original bulb growing in a pot on his mantelpiece while he was listening to the BBC news on his secret radio. Suddenly he heard the Gestapo outside searching houses for such a radio. He quickly hid his under the floorboards, and the Gestapo never found it. As soon as they were gone he turned on the radio again, just as the news was ending with the announcer saying, '. . . and this was Joseph Macleod reading it.'

'Ah,' said the Dutchman, 'I'll celebrate this moment by calling my little daffodil Joseph Macleod.'

It was a lovely March day with a summer sun

shining, and as I wandered around picking, Cherry performed her own wandering, a sniff here, a sniff there.

A fence of posts and lengths of wire divides the bulb field from that of a farm and, when reflecting upon what might have happened to Cherry, I remembered seeing her for a moment pass under the wire, and sniff the grass in the farm field, perhaps even nibble it. There was no question of any weed-killer substance being sprayed there, but it was the time of year when nitrogen was sprayed. Nitrogen is perfectly harmless once it is left in the open for a short while, but manufacturers do warn that it can have unpleasant gas-like effects when it is handled unless dealt with with care. So perhaps this was the cause of Cherry's illness. Perhaps the tractor I had heard in the field a half an hour before had been spraying nitrogen, and Cherry had been unlucky enough to inhale its fumes. No one was at fault. Fate decided me to go and pick the Joseph Macleod daffodils when I did, and for Cherry to follow me. Her recovery was slow, though it seemed to be a complete one. I say 'seemed', because there was to be a recurrence; and the poison theory was then solved.

As a reward for my nursing, Cherry proceeded to make a special fuss of me. I felt embarrassed. I felt like a single parent, or a parent who only makes token visits to their children, because I, in return, did not have the time to make the same measure of fuss of her. I had to push her off my typewriter when she didn't want to be pushed off. I had to push her off my lap when the gas on the stove had to be turned off, or when I wanted a pencil just out of reach, or my spectacles. As a single parent I had no one to ask to do the tasks for me.

She was also unexpectedly charming to strangers, as if she was wanting everyone to join the celebration of her recovery. Instead of hiding, and earning such remarks as, 'Bet she will appear after we've gone,' she would appear on cue when I called her; and when she appeared on the patio called the bridge, just as a photograph was being taken, she was greeted with much praise. She modestly accepted the praise.

It was after her recovery that Cherry initiated a new ploy. Around ten o'clock of an evening she demanded that I should go to bed. Instead of leaving me alone and finding sleeping quarters elsewhere, she would jump on my lap, off my lap, on my lap, off my lap, and if I did not respond she would stalk into the bedroom, position herself at the window, staring down the lane towards Monty's Leap. Maybe she was wanting to go out into the darkness, but this proved not to be the case. Anyway she could not get out of the window although it was open. I never wanted her to go out at night, and so I kept in place the wood and wire contraption that Jeannie and I had made to stop Monty going out in the early days. She would wait there until I did go to bed, then she would stretch, jump on the bed, and take up a position which was sure to give me discomfort.

Such a gesture of affection was a mixed blessing.

I was of course flattered; and I was ready, at any rate for a while, to pay the price for such flattery. Soon, being tired, I would fall asleep unperturbed by her cramping presence, content to pay the price that has to be paid for a cat's flattery. I am inclined, however, to be a three-o'clock-in-the-morning person, who awakes at that hour when problems have a habit of enlarging themselves, of becoming ever more complicated and worrying. I would lie trying to unravel the complexities which were embroiling me, while Cherry in deep sleep, having staked a place in the middle of the bed on my knees, pinioned me into immobility. There I was yearning to toss and turn, but I had to lie straight as if tied to a plank.

This situation is familiar to those who have a cat; and so too what often follows. As I lay pinioned, there would suddenly be an eruption of purrs, and as there had been no special contact between us, the cause of the eruption could only have been due to a benign dream. Action followed. A gentle kneading, that subtle form of contentment, accompanied by an increasing volume of purrs, a Philharmonic orchestra of purrs. Such music amidst my three-o'clock-in-the-morning worries was soothing to listen to, until there was a threatening development.

Cherry would decide to change her position on my knees, and advance, purring, towards my face. Inch by inch, kneading all the while, claws kneading the blanket, she would reach a point where the blanket offered no further protection for me. Only the top cotton sheet protected my neck and my face.

At this stage a ruthless decision would have to be made, and the decision was understandably fudged by the flattery of Cherry's attention. In this situation I would decide to manoeuvre my body, swivelling it gently, so that I would be in a position to pick her up, and remove her to a safe part of the bed. In theory it seemed easy to do. In practice I would find Cherry purring more loudly than ever, kneading more energetically than ever, as if she believed that my movements were on her behalf not mine. However uncomfortable I might have been, how could I summon the courage to remove her?

I would continue, therefore, to lie immobile, Cherry would continue to purr and to knead, and my three-o'clock-in-the-morning thoughts would continue to revolve in my mind. As always they criss-crossed in unruly fashion. One line of thought would suddenly be interrupted by another. There would be chaos in my mind, and what so vexed me was how such disturbing thoughts predominated. Here I was in this lovely old cottage where there had been so much happiness, writing imaginary letters to those who had upset me, vitriolic letters which never saw the postman because daytime cooled me.

IV

I was in the mood to be with the donkeys, and I
collected carrots, and was about to leave the porch
when I saw the General preening himself by the
escallonia. I picked up the tin containing grain and
threw him a couple of handfuls. He responded with
a resonant croak, and a drumming of wings. He
was not alone. His harem were with him: six humble
spotted brown lady pheasants who had been conquered by the charm of the General in the spring.

I had christened him the General a year before.
I did so because of his splendid, authoritative
appearance which reminded me of British Empire
days, and Colonial Governors who wore such col-
ourful uniforms to impress the natives. The General's uniform was particularly magnificent. There
were the burnished copper-coloured feathers of his
body, the metallic dark green head and neck, the
bright red wattles around the eye, and the long
tail, so long that one might think it was an inconvenience rather than an asset.

'Stay around, General,' I said, 'I won't be long,
and I'll give you some more.'

I left him with his harem and walked on down the lane, across Monty's Leap, and on to the Solitude gate where Merlin and Susie were standing close by.

Both Merlin and Susie are, one might say, deputy donkeys. Merlin came to keep Fred company after Penny had died. Susie came to keep Merlin company after Fred had died.

It took a while to find Merlin, months in fact. We kept following up advertisements but none of the donkeys advertised were suitable for one reason or another. At last I saw an advertisement in the Donkey Breed Society News Letter:

MINGOOSE MERLIN, large dark brown eighteen-months-old registered gelding by ROMANY OF HUNTERS BROOK, ex prize-winning mare. Very successfully shown, excellent potential for driving. Kind, knowledgeable home for this exceptionally handsome and lovable donkey my first consideration. Mrs V. Bailey, Skinners Bottom, Redruth, Cornwall.

We had a date next day for a minor check-up on the Volvo, and we had to go to Kessells, the garage at Penryn, and I said it would be a good idea to go on afterwards to Skinners Bottom. After the Volvo had been checked, we went to have a drink at the Greenbank Hotel facing the estuary at Falmouth. It is a legendary hotel where sea captains of the Windjammers used to stay after their long journeys across the oceans. It is a hotel of sentimental memories for me. During the first few weeks of the Hitler war I was a private in the Duke of Cornwall's Light Infantry, and I was stationed at Pendennis Castle overlooking Falmouth Bay. No bath facilities there. I used to go to the Greenbank for a bath.

The Greenbank has one special claim to fame. Kenneth Grahame was staying there when he first had the story idea of *Wind in the Willows*. While staying there he began a series of letters to his son, the date being May 1907. The first two letters are in the possession of the hotel, and they are on display. One begins, 'My darling mouse'. Another, 'Have you heard about Toad?', and then Grahame goes on to tell a story.

We had our drinks, then I telephoned for an appointment with the owner of Mingoose Merlin at Skinners Bottom. An hour later we had met Mingoose Merlin for the first time; and this is what happened:

The sellers were a young couple who didn't want to sell him but they had another donkey, an old donkey, and Mingoose Merlin, a year old, was too rumbustious a companion. He had come to them from a nearby donkey breeder Jenifer Hilliard of the village of Mingoose, hence the name Mingoose Merlin. We also learnt that the name Mingoose Merlin was chosen as being a dignified name for his entry into the Donkey Society Stud Book. Mingoose Merlin, however, was Merlin to his friends.

We proceeded from the house to be introduced, and on the way I explained that we were not wanting to buy him for ourselves but only as a companion for Fred. 'Would it be possible to have him on a week's trial?' I asked cautiously, 'just in case they don't get on together?' We reached the stable yard.

'Merlin!' the about to be ex-owner called out.

And Merlin appeared.

He bounced up to the fence like a dog wagging its tail, pushed his nose into my hand, then into Jeannie's, and skedaddled away out of sight around a farm building.

'Merlin'! came the call again, anxiously, like a mother wanting a child to be on its best behaviour.

Merlin had other things to do. But we had seen enough. His breeder had said that he was the most lovable donkey she had ever bred, and we believed her. His brown coat was long and shaggy, and Jeannie, laughing, said he looked like a yak. The coat half covered his face, and it covered his legs so that it looked as if he were wearing old-fashioned plus fours.

Ten minutes later Mingoose Merlin was ours.

He arrived in a horsebox on the following Wednesday. He had had experiences of horseboxes. He had been a show donkey, third in the foal class of the Bath and West Show, best foal at six weeks in the Penzance Show, best foal at the Devon County Show. All of this coming under the guidance of his breeder. It was a glamorous beginning to his life. It disturbed Jeannie and me a little that by coming to us, his show days were over.

Conventional show days that is. He was scheduled to have, however, many, many private show days, and still does.

Fred and Merlin had instant happy companionship. So also was the case when, a year after Fred had died, Susie arrived to join Merlin. I had been on my own for six weeks, and so it was inevitable that my mind had dwelt more and more on Merlin's situation. He had loved Fred, and when Fred had been taken away he let out a great wheezy bellow. Merlin has never been able to bray in usual donkey manner.

So I decided to find him a companion, and once again the Donkey Breed Society came to my help. The local secretary had bred this donkey called Susie who had spent the first five years of her life in a field close to the fire station at Truro. Then she was sold to a lady near Bodmin, and the lady was selling Susie because Susie did not like the goats the lady had on her holding. I bought Susie unseen; and when the day of her coming to Minack arrived, I was a little on edge. How would Merlin, a gelding, react to feminine company? I had had, however, a taste of his attitude.

During the year he was on his own, he fell in love with a donkey called Nellie of the neighbouring farm. Only a stone hedge separated them at one point, and here Merlin used to stand, hour after hour, hoping that Nellie would appear. She was a little donkey, grey like Susie proved to be, but she was a flirt. I would watch as she came up to the low stone hedge, watch Merlin's delight as she pushed her nose across the hedge to him, and then provocatively scamper away. A most unsatisfactory relationship for Merlin, but he loved her. Then came the day I heard that Nellie was ill, so this was the reason that Merlin had been standing alone by the hedge. There followed an extraordinary incident.

I used to bring Merlin back to the fields around the cottage at night so that he had the stable to shelter in. The gate was held fast by a chain looped in a knot. There was another gate close to Monty's Leap, which was also held fast by such a chain. There came a morning when I found both gates open ... and no Merlin. This is what had happened.

Merlin had miraculously undone the chains, then gone up the lane, past the farm at the top, and along the quarter of a mile to the main road. But he did not go on the main road. He turned right along a minor road until he came to the turning by the old chapel, the turning to Nellie's farm. Merlin had never walked that route in his life. How does one explain this? Nellie had died.

On the day of her arrival, Susie disembarked from her horsebox at the farm, and was led down the lane by her escort. It was a terrible day, drenching rain. I was waiting by the Solitude gate, Merlin beside me, waiting apprehensively. Then I saw this tiny donkey attached to a halter:

She looked like a toy whose child owner had drowned it in the bath. Her legs made me think of

55

matchsticks, and I thought how easily they could
be broken. Had I made a mistake? Merlin didn't
think so.

Merlin had gone berserk. Merlin on the other
side of the gate was prancing like a see-saw, and
making that weird noise which is the best thing he
can do to emulate a proper hee-haw. I undid the
gate, opened it ajar, then, her halter off, Susie
entered the field. Bedlam!

Off raced Susie, Merlin in pursuit. Round and
round they went, back legs flying, hoots from Susie
. . . all this as the rest of us stood laughing in the
rain. Then Susie came at speed towards us, put on
her brakes, slid, and pulled up beside the gate,
puffing. Behind her came a lumbering Merlin, who
looked huge in contrast to her.

I gave Merlin and Susie their carrots, saw a fox
slide along the far end of the field, noticed a
Newlyn trawler sailing west, and was vexed with
myself that I hadn't brought a biscuit with me
because the robin, emblem of Jeannie, and who
always appears when I am feeding the donkeys,
was hopping around impatiently. Then I felt in
my pockets and, thankfully, found a few crumbs.
I left, and went back to the cottage where the
General was still present, along with his harem.
A pheasant is not just a sex symbol to his harem.
He is their protector against predators, a protector both of the ladies themselves, and their nests.
I was often to watch him on guard. He would
wait until his ladies had had their fill of grain,
and only then would he peck at it himself; and

this usually meant I had to throw him an extra handful.

He etched his presence slowly into my consciousness. At first I felt surprise at his occasional arrival in the neighbourhood of the cottage. He might be absent for weeks, then I would be alerted by his vibrant few seconds' call, and I would see him in the shadows of the escallonia. I would toss him crumbs from the bread I kept for the gulls, and when he did not show much interest in such crumbs, I went to a pet shop, and asked what could be recommended to please a wandering pheasant. I returned with a bag of maize, corn, peanuts and sunflower seeds ... and from that day the visits of the General became regular; and I became curious to know more about his wanderings.

My first clue came when I saw him one late afternoon by Monty's Leap. I was standing by the waterbutt outside the cottage, and from that distance I could see only the outline of his shape. I half hid myself, then watched him coming up the lane, and as soon as he came closer I noticed he had a limp. He reached the cottage, and I proceeded to throw him his grain.

The second clue came a week or two later when I was standing by the Solitude gate at the entrance to Oliver land. I was standing there giving Merlin and Susie tea biscuits, and Cherry had come up the lane with me, and she was sitting in the lane watching. She often came with me to feed the donkeys ... 'the donkey girl', I would call her on these occasions. The blue packet of tea biscuits was

nearly empty when I suddenly saw, at the far side
of the field by the gap which led to the honeysuckle
meadow, the figure of the General coming towards
us. He did not come very far. He returned to
the gap as soon as he was aware of the activity at the
gate. But his appearance had helped me with the
mapping of his movements. From then on I often
noticed him crossing the field, and I was able to
establish his route to the cottage ... across the
field, up the lane and over Monty's Leap, and back
the same way. He seldom flew. Sometimes, if
startled in the neighbourhood of the cottage, he
would take to the air, making loud protests as he
did so, but normally he stayed on the ground,
running very, very fast indeed when he chose to do
so. Why did he not regularly fly? Folklore has it
that pheasants do not fly unless forced to do so.
Instinctively they know they are in danger if they do.

The General, I now realize, was reconnoitring
the area for his harem, and as soon as he had
decided that Minack was to his satisfaction his
harem began to arrive, one by one until there were
six. The escallonia was the lure. It gave splendid
cover and although it was never to be used as a
roosting place, it was ideally designed as a restaurant. Hence, despite the foraging around the cottage
during the course of the day, the main meal took
place in the restaurant about a couple of hours
before dusk. I would throw handfuls of grain into
the escallonia. The harem would peck, the General
would watch; and he had in particular to watch the
magpies.

Magpies have dramatic personalities, and I would favour them, court them in fact, were it not for their ferocious appetite for eggs and small birds. Once upon a time they were a comparative rarity, and there was the saying 'See one magpie bad luck, see two magpies good luck'. But today they are becoming in many areas as common as pigeons and so, in order to play a part in their control, I try to seek out their nests, then remove their eggs. I set out to find such a nest one April morning when the harem had begun to arrive.

I had chosen to search the small wood that borders, on one side, the field where we grew Early Bride, Barrett Browning, and Actaea, all of them white narcissi which come into bloom after the yellows are over; and it is also close to the field where the scented yellow California abound, and where we built the greenhouses in those first years of enthusiasm.

I set off from the cottage across the donkey field, so called because it was the favourite field of Penny and Fred when they were here, and where they liked to stand at its edge, staring down at us as we sat in the porch, willing us to pay them attention. It was also the field where Fred had his first birthday party and where at another birthday party occasion the proceedings were filmed for the BBC's *Look Stranger* programme.

I had gone three quarters across the field, had passed the section of the wood on the right where for decades there had been elms which had now been devastated by elm disease, and was at the point where their neighbours the ash trees reach triumphantly into the sky, bare of leaves because of the time of year but free of disease ... when I glanced back, and, weaving through the grass towards me, saw Cherry. A Cherry who was now well enough to join me. It was a delicious moment. I had no idea where she was when I set out, but from some hide she had seen me leave, and instinct made her wish to be with me.

I reached the meadow which runs alongside the wood. It was a bog when first we came to Minack, but there came a time when we decided to reclaim it, and plant daffodils there. It was a plan that was easy to talk about but backbreaking to put into practice. We had Tommy Williams, a lanky, eccentric Cornishman, helping us, and he proceeded to dig five ditches along the length of the meadow, parallel to each other, a task which today, with a bulldozer, would have taken half an hour. It took him a fortnight.

Occasionally I would help him, but a couple of hours was enough for me, and I would retire back to the cottage. One morning I was digging away when Jeannie appeared with the news that Alan Whicker was at the cottage with a television crew. It was the period when *A Gull on the Roof* was about to be published. On that morning I followed Jeannie back to the cottage, the long Cornish shovel balancing on my shoulder, thankful that I had been relieved of my tedious job of digging. I remember little of the interview which followed except for a question he asked each of us separately out of earshot of the other.

'What do you quarrel about?' was the question.

A reasonable question, I suppose, when a couple accustomed to a hectic sophisticated circle find themselves alone with each other for twenty-four hours a day.

'We don't!' Jeannie had replied.

Not quite true. We quarrelled over small matters.

Having dug the ditches, we laid earthenware drain pipes along each ditch but then we came up against a problem. It was necessary before filling the ditches to lay stones along either side of the pipes and over the gaps where each length of pipe joined; this was to prevent the earth from seeping in and clogging the pipes. But we hadn't enough stones. What could we do?

'Periquita!' cried Jeannie suddenly as we were discussing the problem, 'and we'll get rid of the bottles!'

Periquita, a Portuguese wine, then cost 30p a bottle, and it was a favourite of ours. Over a long period the pile of empty bottles had mounted into a hillock. The dustmen who collected the dustbins at the end of the lane a mile away wouldn't take them. The sea was an alternative but bottles in the sea could be dangerous.

'Brilliant, Jeannie!' I said.

And it was thus that the meadow beside the wood which I had now reached, Cherry behind me, became known as the Periquita meadow. Beautiful yellow daffodils blooming in early spring above. Empty bottles below.

I sat down on a lichen-covered granite rock, and I felt the peace of being alone. A woodpecker called, and I wondered in which, among the fallen elms in the neighbourhood of Minack, it had decided to have a nest. Much effort required. Tap, tap, tap with the beak, slowly, painfully perhaps, creating a hole in the chosen tree.

Cherry, who had been at my feet a moment ago, had disappeared. I was in the mood for her company. I wouldn't have wanted the company of a human being. Wonderful exceptions occur, of course, when one is in tune with someone, so freshened by 'the exquisite pleasure of being understood without laboriously having to explain' that one relaxes in a glow of confidence. There are no inhibited gaps in conversation and when there is a silence, the silence is not a self-conscious one. You are feeling beauty together.

Yet an animal who lives with you can take such a person's place if need be. An animal can represent a father confessor. Instead of talking to a person who is the dustbin of people's sins, real or imaginary, you unload your problems to a creature which mirrors innocence. You speak aloud and no one is there to hear what you say. You pour out your secret thoughts, and the burdens of doubt, guilt, worry, fear, begin to fade. I have often talked in such a way to Monty, Lama, Penny, Fred, Oliver, Ambrose, Merlin, Susie and Cherry. I have felt better for it. I feel I have been in communication with Creation, the natural world which God meant it to be before God became a political football.

Those who worship Creation do not rely on the trappings of organized religions. They feel free. They are spared sectarian conflicts. They can love their neighbour without concerning themselves as to which religion their neighbour belongs.

I sat on the rock, and called out: 'Cherry! Cherry!'

Not a sign.

Here I was in the mood for talking to my animal confessor, and she had deserted me.

A rogue daffodil here and there was still in bloom but the rest were allowing the foliage to outgrow them, their once gorgeous petals now a messy brown. They were the same daffodils that we had planted after we had reclaimed the meadow. They had never been much of a success. I suppose, despite our draining efforts, the ground was still too wet for them.

'Cherry! Cherry!'

I continued to wait for her return; and I found myself wondering how it was that I had become a flower grower. I had never wished to be a knowledgeable gardener. I had no wish to learn the Latin names of plants. Indeed I was not particularly interested in knowing the normal names of plants. I loved the look of them, the scent of them, the wonder of them but, for the details, I did not bother. One can see evidence of this attitude today around the cottage. It is all higgledy-piggledy. The pretty flowers of weeds are the neighbours of conventional flowers. No garden snobbery. Weeds and flowers are equal.

'Cherry, Cherry!' I called again.

And suddenly she appeared, and jumped on my lap and began to purr.

It is a secret little wood. No one ever has come there except ourselves and those we bring. It is the wood where I always hear the first chiff-chaff of the year, boasting its arrival after its long journey from Africa with a repetitive call: 'Chiff-chaff, chiff-chaff!' I remember hearing its call for the first time, that first spring when Jeannie and I came to Minack. I had been city-orientated. My ears had been deaf to the variety of bird songs; and suddenly I heard this call from a tiny bird who had buffeted its way across seas and desert to Minack . . . and on hearing it I was overwhelmed by a sense of freedom.

I sat there, Cherry purring, pondering upon the uselessness of this little wood in modern terms. A developer would bulldoze it, a farmer would let loose his cattle into it, cattle that would stamp it into destruction. It is not so much developers that I fear will destroy remote corners of countryside: there are enough regulations to check them and to give a chance for a formal inquiry to be held. Farmers do not have such stiff regulations. Hence thousands of miles of ancient hedges are being destroyed in Britain so that farmers in their giant tractors can go faster up and down the land. An inquiry, had a regulation demanded it, might have probed the financial background of such destruction. Has this destruction been done only for a matter of convenience? Or is there a real justification for it? There is an ancient circle of stones near here called the Merry Maidens dating back two thousand years. Rumour ran through the district recently that a request had been made to remove the circle to the side of the field. Its ancient position, in the centre of the field, was in the way of the tractor. I was myself, a few months later, to be faced with a similar farming attitude; which concerned ancient croft land, for centuries an untouched safe haven for nature, adjacent to the twenty acres that Jeannie and I had assigned for ever as a nature reserve.

Cherry jumped off me, and began to meander towards the earthen bank which edged the wood, and over which I could see the well-worn trail of a badger path. Cherry weaved her way through the tall daffodil stalks, went out of sight for a while, then I saw her again on the earthen bank, taking a leap after that on to the branch of an elder tree. She stretched, clawed the bark, and looked upwards, deciding whether it was worthwhile to climb further. And she did so decide.

I was about to follow her into the wood on my business of looking for a magpie nest when I spotted at the far end of the meadow, on the very top of the last elm which was still standing out of a group of a dozen or more, a large black bundle of sticks. Automatically I classified it as a carrion crow's nest, and the sight of it made me annoyed. Carrion crows are enemies of the local bird population just like the magpies. However they have an advantage over magpies in that their nests are always so high up that they are almost impossible to reach even by using a long pole. This particular nest was certainly too high to reach, so I realized I was defeated. I might find a magpie nest but the carrion crow family would still remain.

Then, just as I was moving off, I saw a large bird descend like a helicopter on top of the tree and settle into the heap of sticks. It was a buzzard. I suppose I should place the buzzard family in the same category as the carrion crow. They chase small birds but they do not pillage their nests. They search for rabbits and rodents, and perhaps a rogue buzzard may attack an ailing lamb, but for me these matters are excusable. I love the grace of a buzzard. I love its soaring flight, the way it floats in the air pushed by the eddies of a silent power; and I love its wistful mewing cry, eerily echoing high above the landscape, remote from the restless world beneath. I had always hoped that a buzzard would nest at Minack. A couple of years ago, a buzzard pair, of which perhaps this buzzard was one, built a nest in the little wood, forty or so feet up in a tree. They did not stay long. There was a carrion crow's nest not far away, and the carrion crows attacked them, and the buzzards abandoned it. Now, I was thankful to think, there was another chance. This time, perhaps, two young buzzards would grow up at Minack.

It was not to be. A couple of weeks later a ferocious westerly gale blew the tree down. The nest, with two smashed eggs, lay among the dying daffodil foliage. But why had the buzzard chosen an elm tree, the last of the standing disease-stricken elm trees? I had always liked to imagine that birds had an intuitive instinct as to what was safe or not for their nests.

I did not, however, find a magpie nest. I went into the wood, clambering over moss-covered fallen trunks, pausing a while, feeling its ancient solitude, watching a blue tit flitting from branch to branch against the dark background, smelling the damp earth, treading on emerging ferns, everything silent, too soon for the hum of bees, the hum of insects; I was part of a beginning, the lush period lay ahead. I peered upwards and there was no massive bundle of sticks to show me a magpie nest. The pair which haunted Minack had made their nest elsewhere, and I knew that, unless I was very lucky, I would never find it.

'Come on, Cherry!' I called out. 'Time to go home.'

Cherry had not followed me in my wanderings. She had stayed on her branch, contemplating.

'Come on, Cherry!' I called out again.

Cats, I know, do not respond to an order. They prefer to tantalize the caller. They like to stay listening to the ever-increasing impatient, anxious calls that are demanding their presence; and they rejoice that they have such evidence of power. The calls get louder and louder, and still no sign of the cat who is being called. I have learnt, however, the secret of how to counter such selfish cat obstinacy. No doubt many others have also discovered the secret. It is this: after a period of energetic, exasperated calling, stay silent. Be patient. Patience will be rewarded after five minutes or so, and after emotional moments when you have decided you will never see your beloved cat again. But you do. Your beloved cat will smugly reappear.

Thus did I call for Cherry. Thus did she respond in her own good time. And thus did we return to the cottage together.

I had learnt from a book about pheasants that there was an average of twelve eggs per nest and therefore, since the General had a harem of six, there could be seventy-two chicks crowding the restaurant if they all were hatched. There were many hazards, of course, to be faced beforehand. It didn't matter, for instance, how cleverly the nest was disguised, how dimly the body of the sitting pheasant moulded into the surrounding area: there was always, besides magpies and carrion crows, the threat of a fox which hunted by scent. There was also the vital importance of a diet of insects needed for the chicks before they were mature enough to enter the restaurant. If it was cold, an easterly wind blowing, denying the existence of insects, there was no hope for the chicks. They would die of starvation.

May and early June were warm and damp, and there was no lack of insects, and I began to make jokes to people who called, filling in vacant moments of talk by making a false-sounding joke. One is inclined to make idiot remarks when filling a conversational vacuum.

'It looks as if I'm going to have a pheasant farm

here,' I would say. 'There are seventy-two chicks on the way!'

The materially minded would reply, 'Will your freezer be big enough for them when they grow?'

I am amazed how attitudes change during the course of one's life. Attitudes which seem entrenched in your nature at the time, you find yourself looking back upon with abhorrence. I had no compunction about shooting pheasants when I was in my teens; or duck as they glided in at dusk in marshy meadows in Norfolk where I was staying with a friend. My friend was a Howard, and his family lived at Castle Rising. His mother befriended me, and she used to send me cakes during school terms at Harrow. Later the family had a considerable influence on my life. Sir Charles Howard was the Sergeant at Arms at the House of Commons, and he arranged for a copy of my book on the British Commonwealth, called *One King*, to be included in the House of Commons library. His son, nicknamed Brown, had influence on me in another way, a potentially disastrous way. He was driving a car, me beside him, along the road in the Castle Rising neighbourhood when he began to pass a car on a bend. I yelled at him: 'Stop!' And if I hadn't done so I wouldn't be here to write these words. At the exact moment we would have passed, a lorry came the other way. I still feel a chill when I remember it.

By June I began to expect the seventy-two chicks to arrive at any time, and I made preparations. I purchased special baby chick feed, I cleared the restaurant of debris like broken twigs and fallen escallonia leaves, and then I waited and I waited. The General continued his daily visit, but that of the harem became spasmodic. There was only one which came regularly, as regularly as the General, and so it was easy to give her a name, and the name was Tilly. She was smaller than the other members of the harem, and more chirpy. She used to come busily to the door, show no fear when I opened it, and *demand* that I should feed her. There was, however, a special feature which was charming to watch. She was obviously the General's favourite concubine. At the end of the day, for instance, they would go off together. I would watch them going down the lane, taking their time of course, then across Monty's Leap, and onwards to the Solitude gate, then across the field towards the honeysuckle meadow. I remember Charlie Chaplin and Paulette Goddard ending a movie in that way, the camera watching them at the end of a day walking into the distance together.

Mid June, the end of June, and no sign of any chicks. I became anxious. True, the prospect of seventy-two chicks crowding the restaurant caused me disquiet, but the disquiet was outweighed by the triumph that would be the case if the General's care and watchfulness succeeded.

Then there came the morning when I was lying in bed having my second cup of tea when I heard outside the bedroom window a persistent, gentle cooing noise, broken every now and again by a warbling chuckle. I jumped out of bed to the window which faces the apple tree, and saw a sight that I will always cherish. Under the tree was one of the harem, and around her, like fluttering fallen leaves, five, ten, twelve chicks, and the mother pheasant was busily shepherding them this way and that; then, to my delight, she began to shepherd them up the path towards the waterbutt and the restaurant.

I raced to the porch door, and found that they had passed the restaurant, and were fluttering towards me as I stood with the door open. It was enchantment. The mother was making me feel she had deliberately brought them to see me, playing the role of all mothers, wishing to show them off. I found the baby chick grain I had specially bought in preparation for this occasion, and threw a handful to them, but I think it was an unwise move because the fluttering leaves scattered without the grain touching them, and a minute later they were being shepherded away down the path from the cottage, past the great rock by the apple tree, past the cherry tree, and then under the gate that led to the stable meadow.

I was never to see them again. What happened? I will never know. But the chief suspects were the family of magpies whose nest I never found. Parents and four young had been haunting the restaurant for weeks. Easy for them to trace any pheasant nest. Easy for them to take the eggs or devour the fluttering leaves. I felt sad for the General. The collection of his harem, his watchfulness over them, had been a wasted effort. The failure did not take him away. He continued to come to the restaurant.

V

I woke up one morning in a placid mood. I boiled a kettle, prepared my usual two cups of tea, and went back to bed. I lay there staring out of the bedroom window at Merlin and Susie grazing on the other side of the valley in Oliver land. As I watched, a comical episode took place. A young fox approached Merlin, and Merlin made a token dart at him and the fox retreated a few steps, then approached Merlin again. They were having fun, no harm in it; and as I lay there observing this therapeutic game, I thought of the mass travellers, sardine-squashed in commuter trains travelling to work; and I thought of the phrase Jeannie, through her life, repeated again and again: 'How lucky we are!'

I lay there planning what I should do during the day. I fumbled for a pen and a notepad on the little table beside the bed; and while I was doing so I noticed a wren fluttering about on the window ledge; and the sight of it made me wonder why windows were not made use of by unwelcome visitors like mice. Why, for instance, does a mouse ignore an open window to enter a room, choosing instead to gnaw a hole through a wall? Why do they not take advantage of such easy access? Idle thoughts like that are amusing, when you have the time to have them.

I lay there making my notes. Go to Penzance, I wrote, and collect the new pair of spectacles. Go to Newlyn fish market and stock up with fish. Go to the Tuck Shop in Alexandra Road, and pick up the Sunday newspapers (last Sunday's, for today was Thursday). Get a new film. Go to Jackson's, the village shop in St Buryan, and buy a supply of sliced peaches for my breakfasts, and granary bread, and chocolate mousse packs, and celery, carrots and onions for the gammon I would cook in the pressure cooker at the weekend . . . This list of shopping was not acted upon. After my second cup of tea, and still watching the fox and Merlin playing their game, I decided I had no impetus to go shopping that day. There was no desperate urgency, I persuaded myself, the two freezers were well stocked up, and so there was no reason why I shouldn't put it off till tomorrow, Friday, and if I didn't feel like it then, there was Saturday, but then, of course, Saturday shopping would be crowded; and so I could leave it until Monday.

There was, however, a more immediate list of tasks to draw up. I had a brown folder, on the outside of which I had scribbled: 'For Immediate Attention'. This order, however, had not been obeyed. There were letters in this folder which had remained unanswered for too long. I love receiving letters because they unite the struggle of writing with the individual who understands what one is trying to convey. Here are two people who are on the same wavelength. A secret friendship between two people who have never met except through their minds; and who communicate in privacy. Such a privacy is the secret weapon of the book world.

Yet it is continually contested by the blare of noise, by the neverending news announcements, by the endless appearances of men and women pushing their opinions upon us from the television screen, by the manufactured stories in newspapers, by fictional violence and by real violence, and all this clutters up our thinking processes so that we become puppets mirroring today's vacuous society . . . yet read a book, a Brontë, a Balzac, a Somerset Maugham, a Galsworthy, a Conrad, a Mrs Gaskell, and you remove yourself from the surface world and meet, in privacy, true friends you will never meet in person. The book, not its version on the television screen, is your friend.

There have been two attempts to screen the Minack Chronicles. The first was instigated by a television company which failed to keep its franchise, and so the idea was shelved. Neither Jeannie nor I at the time were in favour of it because it would attract publicity we did not seek; and yet the company was represented by very sensitive producers who might have presented a worthwhile serial. None the less when the company failed to retain its franchise we heaved a sigh of relief.

The second attempt, or the second proposal, developed after Jeannie died. The BBC proposed a major production which would have meant, so the producer involved told me, four or five episodes being produced a year for five years, and the programme would be shown at 9.00 p.m. on Sundays. I reacted as I did with the ITV proposal. I hated the idea and only went forward with the initial negotiations because my publishers naturally saw the material advantages. Such advantages would have been for me, too, but I was wary. I had a clause put into my contract that if I didn't approve the script, neither the BBC nor anyone else to whom the BBC might sub-let the script would be able to carry on with the production.

I didn't approve the script. It had nothing in common with the Minack Chronicles. Instead, it was a jokey kind of story, and with new jokey characters introduced into the story. So I turned it down, and was thankful. Nevertheless I felt flattered that the BBC had shown such interest; and the incident reminded me of the occasion when the poet, W. H. Auden, approached a young man at a party. The young man turned him down. Auden replied, 'Never mind . . . *nice* to be fancied!'

That morning, that morning when I felt in a placid mood, I became practical after I had had my breakfast of sliced peaches from a tin. I lit a pipe, found my spectacles, and went into the spare room where I keep my typewriter, bundles of cards, a pile of envelopes, the folder marked 'For Immediate Attention', a bulging folder marked for filing, and an assortment of papers for which I haven't found a home. That morning I decided to concentrate on the letters I hadn't answered, and, as always when reading them again, I was very moved. They are personal letters, making me feel involved in the writer's life, and I know my replies are always inadequate. I write them by hand, and I only have the time to write a few lines. If there are no interruptions I manage to write a dozen an hour which is not very many, but it takes time to read each letter, then write the address on the envelope plus the postal code number after deciphering the sender's handwriting. The deciphering of the code number always holds me up.

There was one letter in the drawer of my desk which, however, I had never answered, indeed I had never opened the envelope, and I had had it since a month before the Hitler war began. I had been on the verge of opening it many, many times, but I was afraid that it might result in pangs of nostalgia which I did not want to experience.

The letter was from my mother and she had sent it to the address in Tahiti where I had been staying during my tour of the world. I had left the South Seas when the letter arrived, and the letter was forwarded to my next stop-over which was Auckland. I again had left before the letter had arrived, and so it was forwarded to an address in Sydney, and I had left there, too. Then it was sent on to Hong Kong, and it missed me there. I had left no further forwarding address, and so the Hong Kong Post Office, soon to be taken over by the Japanese, kindly returned the envelope to 'the sender'. Thus it was that the envelope, shortly before Hitler invaded Poland, now littered with world postmarks, having first been posted in the hole-in-the-wall post-box in Lusty Glaze Road near our then home of Glendorgal at Porth near Newquay, was eventually handed to me personally by my mother. I remember holding the envelope in my hands and saying that I was not going to open it because it would recreate a capsule of time when time was mine and I was free, and the war might never come.

My mother had recently been much in my thoughts. It is strange how someone who has been so much a part of one's life becomes absent from one's memory, perhaps for a few months, even for a year or so, then returns so vividly into one's consciousness that they come alive again. So had it been with my mother in recent weeks. I found myself constantly thinking of her, seeing her face so clearly that I found myself speaking to her.

My mother had much charm. She had a selfless devotion to my two brothers and to myself and what perhaps I cherished most about her was her infectious enthusiasm. She was wildly enthusiastic, for instance, about a greyhound system I followed at one time; and this was followed by the same enthusiasm when I followed a horseracing betting system developed by an Austrian refugee from Vienna. The refugee had his headquarters in a tiny room in Sackville Street off Piccadilly, and the fact that it was a Sackville Street address gave my mother the confidence that the man was genuine. He was genuine, and we lost no money, but it proved to be an exhausting racing season for me. I had left Unilever, was out of work, and was living in a place called Joubert Studios off the King's Road. It was during the period when I was a deb's delight at night, a young man who had endless invitations to dinners and dances. My Austrian friend's system demanded that I had to change my betting investment after each race. There were no instant results on television. I had to be continuously on the telephone. But my mother did not deter me. As I found out later, she was wanting to rid me of my gambling complex which she sensed was there. She succeeded.

I was the black sheep of the three brothers, in that I was the only one who did not have conventional success at school, and she was therefore prepared to wing me, not that this interfered with her love for my brothers, but because she had the intuition, despite my school failures, that I had a quality which had nothing to do with the passing of examinations. It is a tragedy that in today's world her intuitive confidence in me would have had no effect. Today I would have had to pass an examination to become a journalist, and I was always incapable of passing any examination. I failed all my examinations at Harrow, but I was still, at the age of twenty-four, able to be chosen to write a column on a national newspaper with advertisements in London buses acclaiming: 'Read Derek Tangye'. A transient achievement maybe, but it was

achieved. The family was surprised. My mother
wasn't. And it could never happen today.

My mother adored Jeannie. She described Jeannie as a 'pocket Venus', saying to me after her first
introduction that she was the prettiest girl she had
ever seen; and, as always when two people are on
the same wavelength, the age difference did not
matter. She was loved too by my two elder brothers, Colin and Nigel, and of course by my father;
and so it was easy for me to bring Jeannie into the
family. 'Why don't you two get married?' Nigel
demanded, on taking us out to lunch after Jeannie
and I had been together for some while; and he
put the thought into my mind. And in due course
Colin, the oldest, the kind, thoughtful Colin, was
best man.

I had been thinking, as I have said, much of my
mother, and that morning when I was feeling
placid I decided the moment had come for me to
open the envelope which had travelled around the
world to reach me and which had waited through
decades and a world war before it was opened. I
thought how strange it was going to be when I
opened the envelope, and touched the writing
paper which last had been touched by my mother.
I decided I would wait until lunchtime, then I
would open a bottle of wine, sit on the sofa which
has been a part of all my adult life, and read. What
would my mother have written to me about all
those years ago?

This ideal situation did not materialize.

I was in the spare room, determined to carry out

my intention of thanking those who had sent me
letters, when I heard the familiar distant knock of
someone at the porch door. Such a knock, however,
can be deceptive. I have on many occasions leapt
to my feet calling 'Coming, coming!' only to find
that it is the gull demanding my attention. On the
other hand there have been times when I have
ignored the knock, believing it was the gull . . . and
the visitor has gone away.

On this occasion, when I heard the knock, I left
my letter-writing and, calling out that I was on my
way, went to the porch; and found a charming
American woman from Texas at the door.

'I feel very nervous arriving here uninvited,' she
said, then added, 'I feel sure you must get tired of
people calling and interrupting you.'

This defensive remark is sometimes made, and I
am never quite sure how to answer it. If I answer
in a serious way I risk the possibility of sounding
pompous. If I make a joke of it I risk sounding
frivolous. I therefore endeavour to be natural by
saying what I truly feel . . . that it is an evergreen
privilege to share Minack with those who, though
living far, far away, have become involved, and are
prepared to come nervously down the winding
lane, and across Monty's Leap.

The American woman was a schoolteacher. She
was elegant, easy to talk to, and showed an intimate
knowledge of Minack life over the years. Except
for one matter.

'How is Jeannie?' she suddenly asked. 'Is she
around? I would so love to meet her. I admire her so.'

'She has died,' I said.

There was a horrified look on the woman's face. She held her hands to her face and broke into a cascade of sobs. I looked away from her, pretending I hadn't seen anything, then relented and said to her in what I hoped was a natural voice, 'I love emotion, I love people who show emotion.'

Yet when I write about emotion, I feel inhibited. I have an irking sensation that someone is looking over my shoulder laughing at me, laughing too at those who display emotion. And it is a quirk in me that I vision the someone to be very clever, someone of high intellectual ability, who has the qualifications to join the influential élite . . . but who has no knowledge of the pulse of real life. Such a person may have power but no warmth. He exists on the surface. On the other hand the someone may not be clever at all. Just stupid, unable to embrace the pain of tragedy. Or the someone may be embarrassed by emotion, thinking it shameful to show it. Or the someone may condemn emotion as evidence of sentimentality. I have never understood why sentimentality is considered a dirty word. For sentimentality reflects love, not violence.

I have had letters of emotion from all over the world since Jeannie died. Again and again people have written saying that they felt they had lost a close friend despite the fact they never met her in person. And on those who knew her she left such a vivid impression.

'I was a child when the two of you came to

supper with my parents,' said a young wife the other day, 'and how she looked has remained vividly in my mind ever since. The figure of a chorus girl, dark hair falling to her shoulders, her clear eyes and her smile ... and the charisma! She looked like a film star, and I would have gone to see every movie she was in!'

Then there were John le Carré's words in his address at her Memorial Service:

> All her life, it seemed to me, Jeannie wore the unmistakable, almost Churchillian air of a beautiful well-bred English girl who was ready any time to hop into a siren suit and do some perfectly filthy job. All her life she remained ready to roll up her sleeves for her friends, who included the animals, for whom she had a magic touch, and the countless readers, fans and odd bodies for whom she always had the time ... The champagne girl. The Savoy girl. The girl about town, with a distinctly modern way of selecting her pleasures ... She could bubble away for hours. Or she could share with you the solid companionship of silence, and let the cliff do the talking. But she knew the rules. She was a child and died a child. She cared for her looks and never lost them.

This impact that Jeannie had on people was to have a mystical consequence which I could not have foreseen.

The first evidence of this was an incident I have described in *The Evening Gull*. It was an eerie incident. A couple called Carol and George Venus who lived in Winchester felt suddenly compelled to come one weekend to Cornwall to find where Jeannie lived, because they had just finished reading *Jeannie*. They found themselves, after a series of strange changes of plan, at the point of Carn Barges whence they could see the cottage, just as Jeannie and I saw it for the first time. There was no one else about.

Suddenly Carol heard shouting, which appeared to be coming from the sea. Then she looked towards the cottage across the croft land in the distance, and she saw a figure. Her husband put his binoculars towards it, and said it was a girl with her hair tied back and a scarf around her neck, and she was waving.

A few minutes later her husband had switched the binoculars towards the cliffs and the sea, because there was still this crying of voices . . . then suddenly he saw the upside down white hull of a small boat, a few yards away, as it turned out, from the rock pool where we used to bathe, and there were three little black blobs clinging to it. Then he switched the binoculars back to the mainland and the girl was still there (I later identified the spot as being in the stable meadow just in front of the cottage). What were they to do? Amazingly a young jogger appeared, and they asked him to race across the land to the cottage in the hope that I could help. And I could. A week previously I had taken possession of a radio telephone, and I was able to call up the Coastguard, and within a very short time a rescue helicopter from the Culdrose Royal

Naval Station arrived, and the three black blobs were rescued. Carol and George Venus looked towards Minack again. The girl was no longer there. Who was she?

I had seen no one. Was it Jeannie? Whoever she was, had it not been for Jeannie making Carol and George feel compelled to come to Carn Barges that weekend, and at that particular time on the Sunday afternoon, those three people would have died.

The second mystical incident occurred three or four months later, at Christmas time.

Special friends, a couple who lived nearby, called to wish me a happy Christmas, bringing a huge box of chocolate biscuits. I sat there thanking them, then talking about the weather, and other trivial matters, when the wife, a very sensitive person, suddenly said, as if passing on a message, that a friend of hers, a medium, had had a visit from Jeannie.

I appeared to remain composed, as if Jeannie had called upon someone on the way home from her regular Friday shopping.

'Oh, really,' I said, and did not even ask who her friend, the medium, might be.

I sensed that my informant was disappointed by my reaction. She was a gentle person, and she thought she was helping me by passing on the news that the otherworldly Jeannie had been in touch with someone who lived in the neighbourhood, and therefore showing me that Jeannie was in touch.

Such caring can be of help to many people, but

it was of no help to me. Many people can understandably gain much comfort by some message,
however vague, from someone they have loved. I,
on the other hand, and Jeannie too when she was
alive, felt dubious as to whether the message sender
was genuine in the wish to communicate. This obviously is a grey area of mystical experience, and
there is no decisive explanation of how there can
be such communication. On this occasion when I
had been told that Jeannie had been in touch with
a medium, I felt irritated, an irritation which was
also funny.

'Jeannie talking from the other world to a
stranger?' I said to myself. 'What was she saying?
What was she gossiping about? We always kept
our private affairs secret to ourselves!'

Jeannie never set out to mix with people just for
the sake of being with people. She did not have
casual girl-friends. She welcomed everyone who
came to Minack, of course, and was at ease with
them, just as she was at ease with people of her
London years, but she was never one to gossip
with strangers. She chose her intimate friends carefully. Hence it was out of character that she should
approach a complete stranger, a medium in this
case, and talk about herself and ask that a message
should be passed on to me.

She did, however, on occasions like to burble
away non-stop, pouring out a volume of her views
on life; and her favourite occasion for doing this
was when picking daffodils. She would have as a
picking companion Margaret the potter, or Joan

who came once a week to help in the cottage. The daffodil beds were many yards long, three feet wide, and each would take a bed at the bottom of the field, then move up side by side picking feverishly. I would be at another part of the field, and though I would be too far away to hear the words, I would hear a continuous drone, sometimes the drone of Margaret, more often the drone of Jeannie. And later I would ask her, 'What was all that about?' And she would reply, 'None of your business!' To break the monotony of picking it was helpful to have such jokes.

It was now on this day that I was in a placid mood that I had the jolt of the third mystical incident concerning Jeannie. The little red van came down the winding lane as usual on time, and Tony, the postman of the week, greeted me with the usual sort of postman's remark: 'Rain on the way,' he said, trying to appear cheerful. And I, speedily scanning the post, replied in absentminded fashion, 'Awful summer . . .'

I carried the post into the sitting-room and sat down on the sofa, and began opening the envelopes one by one and reading the contents. It was the last one I opened which gave me the jolt. I read it, put it down beside me, contemplated, picked up the letter again, contemplated again.

The letter came from a reader who had called a few weeks previously. I had asked him on his arrival at the cottage my customary direct question: 'What do you do?'

It is a question the reply to which has often been

The path to the cliff

Monty's Leap

Entrance to the honeysuckle meadow

The cottage from the Ambrose Rock

Daffodil time

A path in Oliver land

The sign

Our cliff

Jeannie

to my advantage. I am having a plumbing problem and the reply to my question is: 'I'm a plumber.' Or it might be some legal problem in which I am involved, and the reply is: 'I'm a lawyer.'

Then there was the case of my two large freezers. I had absentmindedly switched them off, freezers which were full of supplies for months ahead, and they were off for four days and nights. As soon as I told my sensible friends about this they advised me to dispose of all the contents into the dustbins. I was loath to do this because not long before I had made an equally stupid, expensive mistake.

I have fresh meat sent to me periodically from a firm in Exeter, and I had always received it by Datapost. I had no knowledge that the sending system had been changed, and that my new consignment was to come by carrier, just as books from my publishers come by carrier. The week I expected the meat, a carrier delivered a large parcel and, without checking its contents, I took it for granted that it contained books. The driver put the parcel into the confusion room, the door of which opens on to the lane.

For several days I forgot about the parcel, becoming increasingly cross that the meat had not been sent. I rang up the firm complaining, but they assured me that the meat *had* been sent, and told me the date. It suddenly dawned upon me what I had done. The parcel did not contain books. It contained the meat. I had not been to the confusion room since it arrived; and I now hurried down to investigate. I opened the door, and there was an awful stink. The rotting meat was only fit for a carrion crow, or a magpie.

I was therefore not in the mood to throw away yet more of my larder, and I longed to find an escape from the logical advice of my friends. I was to find an escape ... a beautiful Bengali girl appeared at the cottage door at the height of this crisis.

'What do you do?' came my usual question.

'I am a biochemist,' she replied, then adding the name of the famous firm for whom she worked.

'My dear,' I replied with great warmth, 'you are just the person I need!'

Thereupon I rushed her down to the two freezers, leaving her there. An hour later she returned. She had checked the contents, the freezers had remained chilled, and everything was safe. My logical friends, when I told them of my good fortune, were sceptical.

'Wait and see!' they warned.

I cooked, I ate ... all was well.

Here I was sitting on the sofa reading the last of the morning's post, and contemplating. There was good reason for me to contemplate. The letter was a surprising one.

My mother's letter would now have to wait.

VI

I continued to sit on the sofa, my mind wandering, remembering things past.

They were dreamy days when we first came to Minack. Escape was possible on limited funds. It was a time when a cottage like ours could easily be obtained, when meat was rationed at 6p per person a week, when beer was 4p a pint, when a postage stamp cost 1p, when petrol was 6p a gallon, when we paid potato or flower pickers 10p a hour, when the flower and vegetable markets were not swamped by airborne produce from all over the world, when there was no television in country parishes, and so families created their own enjoyment. It was a time when houses could be left unlocked, when old people could walk the streets at night without the threat of violence, when unwritten laws were respected, when amateurs like ourselves had the chance to make a living on the land, when freedom was not throttled by countless regulations ... it was a beautiful period of innocence when Jeannie and I began our life at Minack.

It seemed indestructible. We never talked about

the distant future. The future was a tiny spot on the horizon which, we thought, did not belong to us. The present was what counted, and the struggle to maintain the mood of the present . . . the daffodil harvest, the potato harvest, should we expand, invest in a greenhouse, two greenhouses, three, and if we could grow six pounds of tomatoes from each plant, let's calculate how much we could make from four thousand plants. And what about freesias? We could grow freesias during the winter before we planted the tomatoes. And there were lettuces to grow, and iris. They were exciting times, hectic times of planning and dawn-to-dusk work. We were immune to the weather. Gales, drenching rain, baking hot days . . . none of this interrupted our determination to survive. We were happy, in tune with the reality of life, free from the man-designed, computer-controlled way of life that the majority is compelled to follow. We never thought it would ever end. When Jeannie was ill she never thought she was dying. There was no last-minute farewell. Indeed I rejoice that there was no dramatic ending scene, that she was alone in the caring presence of the nuns of St Michael's Hospital because, by not being there, I did not have to suffer the feeling of physical finality.

There was now this spiritual aftermath. The medium who lived nearby who said that Jeannie had contacted her; the incident of the three people being rescued from the upturned boat beneath Minack cliff, the vision by the couple, who alerted the rescue, of the girl standing in the stable meadow, waving, then vanishing. We never thought, whoever died first, of continuing an ethereal relationship. We accepted the power of spiritualism but we both felt we would never use it to reach each other.

We were put off, for instance, by the tantalizing stories of near misses. A voice comes through a medium control and the eager listener is thrilled by remarks that seem to prove that the voice is indeed the dear one the listener wants to talk to. Yet there always seems to be a lack of direct contact, a practical form of contact. The form of contact seems to be like an early morning mist, existing but intangible.

Our personal attitudes also shared the theory that for a departed one to tie themselves to earth life because those they have left behind are wishing to remain in contact could be like the break-up of a love affair . . . the one wants to break away, the other tries to maintain it. However there are a multitude of views on this matter, a mass of evidence that those who have been left have been guided in matters of personal importance one way or another, and so I have no intention of being dogmatic. For I remain puzzled. I remain particularly puzzled because of this letter.

It came from a man in his thirties who had come to Minack a few weeks previously. I had felt very much at ease with him, and he had a young son with him who also was effortless. I asked him, as was my habit, what he did, and he replied that he was a professional astrologer. I said I was wary of astrologers because life was difficult enough without one being warned how it was going to materialize; and he admitted that it was sometimes very hard to warn someone who had consulted him as to what he foresaw. I was impressed by his naturalness and his sincerity. There was no glitter of showmanship. He had a gift. He would never exploit it in showmanship style.

The letter read as follows:

I'm not sure if you'll remember me . . . I came to visit you in May this year. I was the astrologer . . . we had a little conversation about the stars in your secret look-out place overlooking the sea. My little son took a photograph of us together.

I'm really writing to let you know of an interesting development. My wife, who has proven powers of mediumship, was in our garden when she became aware of a special visitor standing nearby, looking at our cat Katy. It was your Jeannie (my wife knew her by her photographs) and they stood silently together for a while. Then she communicated a few things to my wife: that she was travelling the world, visiting all the fans of the Chronicles, also all the beautiful places she'd always wanted to see and hadn't. She wanted us to tell you that she was happy because of this, and that she was with a companion. My wife couldn't quite make out the name but she thought it was somebody close to her in life on earth, perhaps a relation. Jeannie had a far-away look in her eyes as if she was looking out to sea, though we live well inland and she was actually looking over neighbouring back gardens. During their 'conversation' Jeannie sympathized with my wife over a sadness she has, and they felt drawn together by their common love of cats. Jeannie said she's spending also a lot of time with you around her old haunts. Time and space are different to her now. She's shown you she's around still, and will do so again soon.

I put the letter down, smiling to myself. What was Jeannie up to? What was she doing dropping in again on a complete stranger and discussing her private life? So unlike her. And who else was she dropping in to see? Was she sending out such powerful vibrations that mediums felt compelled to draw her to them?

A part of me, therefore, treated the letter as humorous, a part of me was wistful, a part of me found it intriguing, and another part was put in a quandary. How am I going to deal with a Jeannie who is wandering around, space and time no object, visiting people in all parts of the world, passing on information which I thought belonged exclusively to the two of us? And what about my own post-Jeannie relationships? Did she approve? Was she commenting upon them to her medium friends? I began to feel that I was being followed as if by a satellite. There was still an unanswered conundrum, however, which needed to be solved. If Jeannie had the mystic power to talk directly to strangers, why could she not have the power to talk directly to me? Not in a vague fashion, a telepathic fashion, which could be interpreted in any way I wished, but in a direct, practical fashion. I determined to put her to the test; and on that day the letter had arrived, the opportunity occurred to do so.

It had been a warm late August day with a hazy mist, a mist which could not be described as a fog, but sufficient for those who control the automatic fog signal of Tater-du, a half mile away, to let it blare. It had, in fact, been blaring continuously for five days and nights, causing annoyance to all those, including holidaymakers, in the neighbourhood because the blaring was quite unnecessary. In a dense fog such blaring is understandable, but Tater-du will start blaring when visibility is clear. More annoying still is that the clear visibility discloses that there are no vessels in the vicinity to warn.

Such a fog signal is in any case an anachronism in an age of radar, satellite navigation and all the other miraculous inventions that can act as the eyes and ears of those sailing the seas. A fog signal situated on the coast is very unreliable because it is at the mercy of the wind. When, for instance, the wind is blowing in from the sea, the fog signal blows inland.

The few who are in favour of it argue that it is needed for the sake of amateur yacht people because yachts do not always have modern navigational facilities, and even if they do, their owners are not qualified to use them. If that is the argument why not create regulations similar to those that car owners have to follow? Cars have to have brakes, have to pass the MOT, car owners have to pass the driving test, so why are those who sail the seas exempt from such regulations?

There is another factor concerning fog signals like Tater-du. The cost of maintenance in keeping it blaring for hour after hour when there is no fog is enormous. The money spent instead on road blackspots would save many lives.

The opportunity to test Jeannie's spiritual interest in my welfare occurred that night after the letter had arrived. I had made the mistake of giving Cherry a saucer of coley. Too much of it. It was five o'clock in the afternoon, and as soon as I saw her gobbling it I realized I had made a mistake. I should have given her only a spoonful of coley, and then, in an hour or two, she would have wanted a second helping. As it was, the helping I gave her was of a quantity that sent her off to choose a place to sleep outside.

At ten o'clock, wishing to go to sleep myself, I went into the night, calling Cherry. I walked down the lane, I stood on the bridge, I walked up to the washing line, and then down again to the space in front of the cherry tree where a car can park. No sign of Cherry . . . and then my torch lit up a pair of pinprick-size lights outside the stables; and I was so relieved to see her that I cried out: 'Cherry! Now I can go to bed. Follow me back!'

She followed me back, yes, but only to within a few yards of the porch, and then she stopped, as if anchoring her paws in the gaps of the paving stones. I reacted gently. 'Oh, Cherry, don't be obstinate . . .'

There was no response. She stayed anchored ...
and then, when I proceeded to cajole her further,
she scampered away, round the waterbutt and into
the darkness. True, I was frustrated by my lack of
power over her, by the lack of her response to the
love I was showing her, but these were not the
basic reasons why I was so anxious to have her safe
in the cottage, without the fear of her getting out
during the night.

One reason centred around the bully cat who
haunted the farms in the neighbourhood. No one
knew where he came from. He would suddenly
appear in the neighbourhood of a farm, hunting
the area for a few days, and violently attack any
local cat whom he came across. He was a large
tabby cat with white paws, twice the size of Cherry,
three times the size in fact, because Cherry was so
small; and if the bully cat attacked her she wouldn't
have a chance. On this particular occasion when
Cherry was evading my blandishments to come
into the cottage for the night, I was aware that the
bully cat was in the neighbourhood.

There was a more important reason why I
wanted Cherry indoors. After her March illness,
she had had a relapse. And it was a very serious
one. She had gone out gaily one late June morning
soon after she had had her breakfast, and I had
watched her to my delight leaping into the air
trying to catch butterflies, failing to do so, of
course.

I had a sixth sense of concern, however, and
although I went back to have my breakfast, I felt I

should keep a watch on her as soon as I had finished. Hence, after twenty minutes, I went out to be with her, found she wasn't in the immediate neighbourhood, then suddenly saw, in the lane close to Monty's Leap, a curious shuffling movement. I hurried down the lane, then realized that the shuffling movement was that of Cherry. She had had a fit.

A stressful interlude ensued. She was trying to reach the undergrowth at the side of the lane, and I knew that if she succeeded she would disappear within it, and rescuing her would become an impossible task. The vet had already warned me that such a thing could happen, and I had heard many stories of cats disappearing when they had become ill. It had been a nightmare thought that this would happen to Cherry, and so I had been on guard ever since her illness in March.

I bent down and clutched her, and she immediately showed that she was not going to cooperate. She struggled violently, and although this meant I was going to have a very difficult time getting her back to the cottage, I took it as a good sign. It proved that she was not in a state of collapse ... but how was I to carry her if she had no intention of being carried?

The door of the confusion room, the room in the building which was once a stable, and so called because I dump into it everything I do not know where else to place, was twenty yards away up the lane towards the cottage; and I now began to wriggle towards it, my tummy on the gravel, my right hand trying hard to keep hold of Cherry. I edged my way to the door, aware that an empty cardboard wine carton or two were just inside, and if I could get one I would be able, I hoped, to drop Cherry into it, then carry the box to the cottage. There was, however, a major problem first to overcome.

The door of the confusion room was secured by a small padlock, and even in normal circumstances I found it difficult to fit in the small key. In the present circumstances it seemed almost impossible to achieve. One aspect of the situation was miraculous. Normally the key is kept indoors but on this occasion I had it in my pocket. All I had to do therefore was to reach the door and insert the key . . . all I had to do . . .

As I wriggled towards the door Cherry was behaving like a mad cat and I had to grip her so firmly that I felt I might be crushing her. The only alternative was to hold her gently, and she would have escaped and I might never see her alive again. I reached the bottom of the door, still lying on my tummy, and looked up at the small padlock, tantalizingly just within reach but just out of reach for manoeuvring the key into the lock. I brought myself alongside the door, then with my left hand began fumbling with the key. Here was a crisis. I *had* to get the key into the padlock slot. Fail and Cherry would be away . . . and I made one last attempt, Cherry struggling beside me, and there came the wonderful moment when the key found the slot, and I opened the door, and there was the empty wine carton which had brought me twelve bottles of Côte du Rhône, waiting to accept Cherry. I placed her gently into it, folded the cardboard cover over it, and carried it, just as rain began to fall, up to the cottage.

There now began a harrowing period. What was wrong with her? She kept shaking her head, she kept swaying, she had lost her balance; and it was pathetic to watch her trying to jump on a chair; and when she tried to make a nest on the bed of the spare room, I filled the floor with cushions to soften a fall. Then at last the ailment was diagnosed. She was not suffering from poisoning. It was an ear problem. Seeds and mites had delved into her inner ear, and the consequence was the loss of balance, and the fit. Human beings sometimes suffer from the same ailment. The remedy was drastic.

The vet, a charming Irishman, said he would operate upon her in the cottage, and Cherry was put on the sofa and given an injection, and we waited as she went off to sleep.

'Always a bit risky,' said the vet.

For half an hour he meticulously cleaned the ears, showing me the mites and seeds he collected, and when he had finished he said to me:

'It will take a while for her to come round, and I want you to watch her all the time, and if she stops breathing . . . just wiggle her toes.'

'Wiggle her toes?' I replied nervously.

'Yes, that will help her to start breathing again.'

For an hour, and it seemed like ten hours, I sat watching. My eyes were glued to the little heaving movement of her fur. Then suddenly she began to come round. A paw moved, her head was half lifted. She was safe. I knew she was safe; and I went into the kitchen and poured myself a drink.

Her recovery was slow but complete; and a bonus was that she developed a beautiful glossy coat. It was thicker and silkier than ever before. It was as if the ear trouble had been affecting her for a long time, and now that the ears were clean, she felt like a young cat again. But the experience left me more on guard than ever. Supposing I had never seen her at the bottom of the lane by Monty's Leap? Supposing she had a fit when she was out at night? No wonder I now wanted her indoors. No wonder I was vexed when she failed to respond to my pleas. No wonder I wanted Jeannie's help.

'Cherry!' and my tone was still gentle, 'do *please* come in.'

She was out of sight. She had scampered away past the waterbutt, and so I followed with a torch, and the light shone on Cherry sitting on the gravel by the white seat.

'Cherry! Cherry!'

She took no notice.

'Cherry!' I called again, and my voice was rising. 'Cherry, come back!'

Instead of coming back she darted down the lane.

'Cherry!'

After ten minutes I knew I was wasting my time. She was like a teenager out on a spree; it was no use for a parent to expect her to come home. So I returned to the cottage, sat on the sofa, read a story in a newspaper that the interest rate had gone down which would help mortgage payers but harm savers. The age-old financial roundabout.

At that moment I asked for Jeannie's help. Now was the opportunity to believe that her spiritual wanderings had substance. Challenge her to help me, and I would begin to feel, if she responded, that the messages I had received did indeed come from her.

So out I went again into the darkness, torch in hand, calling again: 'Cherry! Cherry!'

Within a minute she appeared. Then meekly followed me indoors. My plea for help had been answered.

A few weeks later there was another strange link with Jeannie. A reader of the Chronicles wrote to me that she was driving to Banbury in Oxfordshire, her husband driving, she in the back seat, a friend who was a medium in the front seat. Suddenly the medium began murmuring that a lady was trying to contact her, then added that the lady was saying her name was Emerald. A few seconds later the medium corrected the name. She said that she had got the name wrong, that the lady had come through to say her name was Everald not Emerald.

My correspondent was the only one in the car who had read the Chronicles. She was the only one, therefore, who knew that Jeannie's full name was Jean Everald Nicol. There was no message.

Later there was another occasion for which I asked Jeannie's help to secure Cherry's presence in the cottage. I did so halfheartedly, disbelievingly, in the manner that people touch wood . . . Minack was included in the BBC *Songs of Praise* programme, and the producer wanted a 'shot' of Cherry in the porch. It was an impossible hope. Cherry hated groups; and the BBC team, of Pam Rhodes the interviewer, the producer Garry Boon, the cameraman, the sound man, the secretary, could have been expected to scare Cherry away . . . but when they appeared, along with their camera and sound paraphernalia, she remained sublimely indifferent. She showed no desire to run away. She posed on the red and white check tablecloth. She even, as a gesture, put her nose to my face.

I was now thinking of my mother's letter again. Soon I would open it. I was ready to do so. The mystical activities of Jeannie had been dealt with or, for the time being, seemed to have been dealt with; and my worries about Cherry had also faded, although I remained on guard. So I realized that any time now, any moment, and without a pre-conceived plan, I would suddenly decide to open my mother's letter.

Readers of the Chronicles continued to call. 'Don't you get fed up with people calling on you unexpectedly?' Often that question. Sensitive people come to Cornwall to catch a flavour of long-ago Cornwall. They watch the sea swirling, touch the rocks of the landscape aeons of years old, rocks that reflect the laughter and the tears; the scent of hay and flowers, wet earth, parched earth, gulls crying above them, robins perching, swallows skimming over them, lizards sunning themselves, bees humming, Red Admirals spreading their wings ... this is what people come to Cornwall for. An antidote, just for a short while, to their fight for survival. Tranquillity, like the interior of an ancient church. Modernity does not offer tranquillity, only restlessness. Do I get fed up with people calling? Inconvenient yes, when I am working, but people usually understand.

The Lager Louts, the two gulls, do not however understand. There are periods when one of them will knock and knock and knock on the glass roof of the porch; and this particular Lager Lout has developed another method of demanding my attention. It is a form of tap dance. It reminds me of past theatrical stars like Fred Astaire and Jack Buchanan who used to tap dance their way around a stage or in a musical movie. My dancing gull, however, had a variation to such a routine. He did not move around the glass roof. He stood still, tapping the glass with his webbed feet and making a sound like that of a roll of miniature drums. Sometimes, if I had not taken any notice of him, if I failed to answer the summons to supply him with bread, biscuits or what have you, the sound of drums would rise to a crescendo, forcing me to stop whatever I might be doing in order to obey him. Indeed as I write this paragraph I hear such a crescendo, and off I must go to do my duty. Such an interruption, when I am working, is much more distracting than an unexpected visitor.

This antic of the dancing gull has a folklore

explanation. It is said that gulls perform such a tap dance on lawns and grass meadows in order to deceive the worms. The poor worms think that the sound of the tap means it is raining, and so wriggle to the surface. The Lager Lout was treating me as a worm.

It had been a glorious day, one of those days when the sea blew its scent inland, and you filled your lungs with it, and a sense of freedom surged through you. I felt happy and relaxed, and two couples had come during the day whose description of their lives and their thoughts had stimulated me. This was one of my rewards, living in a faraway Cornish cottage, and meeting people who experience the rawness of late twentieth-century life, meeting people who shine above their distress. People who have the courage, and it has to be a persistent courage, to face up to such distress. It had been a glorious day, and I now had decided that this very evening I would open my mother's letter.

First I collected it from the drawer in the Regency desk which my mother and father had given us as a wedding present. I took it over to the small table which stands beside the sofa, and I placed it upright against a Wedgwood vase which a friend gave us. I placed it there so that it would look me in the face after I had returned from what I was about to do. It would face me, demanding to be opened. What I was about to do was to give the donkeys their supper.

I walked up the lane to the Solitude gate, bringing with me the usual packet of tea biscuits.

'Merlin!' I called. 'Susie!'

The dying sun was free of clouds, and a dazzling light lit the green field, sharpening it from a dull green to a brilliant green, and burnishing the bracken at the edges of the field from a sombre brown to a copper glow, sparkling the stirring sea; while above me silent gulls, glinting white, floated downwards to the rocks.

'Merlin! Susie!'

I leant against the gate, and I thought of the millions who had spent the day, as Thoreau put it, 'in dull desperation'; and there echoed Jeannie's voice in my mind: 'How lucky we are!' And I went on to think of the circumstances which had led us here, how a sense of destiny had driven us. No intellectual motivation, no conventional self-discipline. Just the happiness that was beckoning, doing what we wanted to do, not stifled by the phrase 'take care'. Disasters we had, and I have listed them in the Chronicles, but they never shook Jeannie or me from knowing that we were doing what we were meant to do. 'Take risks' was our watchword. Not 'take care'.

I heard the sound of galloping hooves way up to the left, then through the gap by the blackthorn alley, first Susie, then Merlin, Susie flinging up her back legs in delight that supper had arrived, Merlin lumbering. Down the field they rushed.

'Where have you been?' I said, pushing biscuits into their mouths. 'I've been calling you for five minutes!'

VII

I fingered the envelope for a moment or two, mar-
velling at its long-ago travels and the places it had
been to stamped upon it. No extra stamp charge
had been made. The envelope had travelled around
the world for tuppençe halfpenny in old money.

I hesitated for another second or two, then at
last slit open the envelope of the letter which was
meant to reach me decades before. This is the
letter:

Darling, once again there's mail advertised for the
Society Islands and here we are in the midst of
Xmas week. Ann and Nigel have already arrived.
We are experiencing such cold as we never remember ... it's been 44 degrees in New York and
England has now got it this week. Two days running our pipes have frozen ... it makes it very
difficult, although we luckily have each time got
hold of our plumber. However so long as the freeze
goes on as fast as we de-freeze the pipes freeze up
again. *So* nice just at Xmas time. Icicles are hang-
ing all over the Island, a most romantic sight. The
wind is so bitterly cold one hesitates a very great

deal about going out. Gib [my father] said this
morning: 'To think of Derek basking in the sun
dressed in shorts.' It certainly is difficult to
imagine in this arctic atmosphere. Audrey is staying a few days with Fildes in Jubilee Place before
coming down here, and she writes the pipes are all
frozen in Jubilee Place too [Chelsea]. Nigel tells
me he's sent you a pound in a letter. I do hope it
reaches you for as he said, he wanted you to take it
out and feel it was there to spend on an extra, so
different to having it placed in the Bank and you
having to draw it from the Bank. It's a charming
idea but in my cautious soul I would feel the
money might go astray, just sent in a letter, so I'm
afraid you won't have any surprises in a letter
from your mother. It's rather absurd because a
letter as like as not will reach you and if it were
not for this innate feeling in these hard times that
it would be bitter if the letter went astray, I would
gladly enclose some of your birthday and Xmas
money. However your movements are too uncer-
tain, and quite likely you'll have left the islands
before this reaches you. Gib says New Zealand is
your next call ... he's sending the £100 there.
However he'll have told you all about that. I don't
know why you think you'd better stay in Australia
a month ... we don't follow why, if you want your
money to reach further because you'll spend a lot
of money there. However you always have your
own firm ideas about things so presumably there
is some reason. It looks as though by the time you
get there, there'll be more crises and Japan may be
at war with us. Really we're fed up with these
continuous situations ... the dictators seem to
have only one idea of life these days and that is

threats of war and now they're hand in hand with Japan, they feel we're threatened at every point, blast them.

Nigel is sitting here at the moment and tells me to inform you that the seawater icicles are ten feet long. I enclose a newspaper paragraph about Jan which will interest you. I can imagine her coming out from a restaurant to find the air so cold which literally came an hour or two after a perfect day, and feeling a new hot-water bottle was a necessity. Colin's new car has been delivered and he's due here on Friday. He's bringing Fildes with him. Much love darling ... we shall all think of you and wonder so much how you will spend Xmas Day. Always lovingly Mum.

I touched the page, and knew that here indeed was a moment when time had stood still. I was young again. My mother was worrying about how I would be spending Christmas Day; and she was telling me, just as if the letter had arrived by the morning's post, who was coming to the Glendorgal Christmas party. Nigel, my brilliant brother, an aviation expert, who designed the flying sequences in the H. G. Wells movie *The Shape of Things to Come*. Ann, Ann Todd, to whom he was married for a while, and whose daughter Francesca, my god-daughter, has won fame in France as an artist. Colin, my eldest brother, kind, reliable, fun, who was bringing Fildes, his godmother, whom my mother had known from childhood days. And then there was Audrey, my mother's sister, an enchanting person, who had shared a house called Rutlands with Fildes in Bushey Heath where, in my Harrow schooldays, I used to stay during the traditional Eton and Harrow match at Lord's ... and for whom I caused much inconvenience: 'What are we going to do to entertain Derek?'

Audrey and Fildes were anchors in the Tangye family. The Christian name of Fildes was Ethel, and she hated it; and so from early on in her life she became just Fildes, but she also had another name by which she was always called by us children, and the name was Gar. I have no idea how this came about. She was a large lady with a wispy moustache, and she had a heart of gold. She was incessantly involved in charity work which she did quietly without expecting recognition, and was always very generous to the family. She was a wonderful listener and if she approved of what one was saying, she would sit still in her chair. If she started gently to sway, one was immediately on guard. She had very decided views about current events and about individuals. For instance, when I met a girl who I thought might be more than a passing acquaintance I would nervously bring her to see Gar; and it was such a relief when the girl passed the test. Gar, in fact, played the role of the matriarch of the family.

Then in her letter my mother mentions Jan, and enclosed a newspaper paragraph about her. 'At three this morning,' wrote a *Daily Mail* columnist, 'I saw a beautiful girl in a white ermine coat buying a hot-water bottle in Piccadilly. Who was she? Miss Janet Johnson, the talented young actress.'

Jan and I had one of those friendships which was close but both knew had no future:

> Sometimes, [I wrote] people come together and ·remain content with each other for a while because their personal circumstances by luck coincide. Soon their friends take it for granted that they are always together, and neither is invited anywhere without the other. It is a soothing time; and yet
>
> both inwardly know they are living on a kind of suspense account. They do not belong to each other. They suit each other for the time being, that's all. They are waiting.

I met her after she had came from Australia to appear in a play at the Criterion Theatre. She later went to Hollywood for a while, and when she returned she was cast as the young girl in Robert Sherwood's beautiful anti-war play *Idiot's Delight* in which Raymond Massey played the lead. The out-of-London run began in Glasgow, and I went there for the first night in my capacity as the *Daily Mirror* columnist, my column being called 'Personality Parade'. I wrote a rave review. Henry Sherek, the ebullient producer, said later that the review and the consequent publicity did much to launch the play's success in London . . . and it also helped to launch Jan as a young star. Five years later there came an echo to this story. Jeannie told me how she had read my review, went to see the play as a result, was captivated by it and saw it, sitting in the upper circle, six times, and as she left the theatre to go home to St Albans, I would have been at the stage door waiting to take Jan out to supper.

After *Idiot's Delight* Jan was chosen to play the lead in a play originally intended for Vivien Leigh. Vivien Leigh was already a star, although her role as Scarlett O'Hara in *Gone with the Wind* still lay ahead. Jan was apprehensive about accepting the chance because she felt she could not follow in the footsteps of Vivien Leigh. However the press greeted her warmly, and it appeared that all was well.

Then, one late night, ten days before I was setting out on my journey round the world, and was about to spend my last few days at Glendorgal, Jan's dresser rang me at my Chelsea mews flat, saying that Jan needed me, that she couldn't face continuing with the part, and that it was up to me to take charge, adding that Jan wasn't aware that she was ringing me.

I cannot remember in detail the way I handled the situation. Just that within a day or two, Jan and I were on the way to Cornwall and Glendorgal.

'We shall all wonder how you spend Christmas Day,' my mother had written. How did I? There I was in Tahiti far, far away from the frozen pipes of Glendorgal. Here are extracts from my diary:

24 December.
I came back to Papeete and am staying at the Hotel Tahiti in what people say is the best room

in the town. It is large, spotlessly clean with a big
balcony, utterly private. I am sitting there now
watching the world go by. There are half a dozen
sailing boats tied up by the wharf just below me,
though the road is in between. And beyond them
is the lagoon, and in the hazy distance the island
of Moorea, and away to the west the sun is beginning to set.

The people look so beautiful. The girls in tiny
shorts and blouses made in the material of the
pareu, in reds and greens and orange. Their black
hair, combed and brushed so that it gleams, falls
down their backs. Their skin is a golden brown;
slim golden brown legs. Sometimes they wear san-
dals, sometimes they are bicycling barefeet. No
hats, only a flower, a *tiare tahiti* stuck behind a
ear.

26 December.

Yesterday was the strangest of Christmas Days. I
lunched with a charming Englishman called John
Hardie and his wife who is Tahitian with lovely
kind eyes. He is a sort of assistant at the Consulate.
He is middle-aged, had a business in Japan until
he was pushed out. He doesn't like the Japanese.
He says they are determined to conquer the world,
using any means to do so.

I met other people at the lunch and afterwards.
There was Monsieur Wilmé with a personality so
quietly peaceful that it was restful to talk to him.
He has a house in Papeete and works for a phos-
phate company. He lives with his *vahine* who is
twenty-one and who has been with him for four
years: 'The natives have minds like children,' he

said. 'I am not in love with the girl but I like her about the place . . . a native husband doesn't mind his wife being unfaithful when he is sober, but he gets angry when he's drunk.'

It was a very warm day, the lazy atmosphere of a summer's day, and after lunch I made a pilgrimage to Loti's Pool. There are two of them. The first had all the appearance of a city park, and I was told to move my bicycle from the grass. But then I went on right up the valley until I found the pool of Raratu. No soul was around, and so on this Christmas Day I bathed in the loveliest pool in the world.

I returned in the evening to Papeete, met a girl with pale blue, slanting eyes. I took her to supper where she told me that her mother was Tahitian and her father French. Such a happy way of ending Christmas Day.

The 'Gib' in my mother's letter was, of course, my father. My parents were so devoted to each other. He was a romantic, and he, too, had travelled the world at around my age; and although he never went to Tahiti, he went to Robert Louis Stevenson's Samoa, and this remained an imperishable memory all his life. Thus he followed my journeys, wrote numerous wonderful letters to me, and lived again this time in the islands of Samoa. He wrote me the following letter from Glendorgal at the time he guessed I was about to leave Tahiti:

I can't resist sending you a line on this your very last day in Tahiti for I know how you will be feeling. It is now about 4 a.m. with you, and you will have had your last dance, and in a few hours the farewell *tiaré* will be round your neck, and you'll be waving farewell and promising to return again. And if you are wise, you never will return again, for it will never be quite the same as this, your first visit. Many a time you will recall memories of the waving palm trees, the sighing of the sea on the reef, the fantastic shapes of the mountains, and the merry maidens' voices. And one day you will somehow and somewhere get a whiff of the scent of the coconut mingled with that of the *tiaré*, and in a flash you will suddenly be transported in spirit back to that happy isle. The memory of it will be a blessing to you for ever.

I would never have been able to write my Tahitian diary had I not been sacked by the *Daily Mirror*. I believed my position was secure, had made plans to tour European capitals, but suddenly I found myself a victim of a palace revolution, and I was out of a job. A bottle of champagne and four hours of thought brought me a solution. I asked my ex-editor's permission to write one more column. Here is the column, flowery, wordy, but to the point. My mother's letter had prompted me to find it. It was prefaced by a cover-up letter to the editor (cover-up for my sacking):

When you asked me to write 'Personality Parade' you gave me a great chance. A chance to help me to reveal something of both the glamour and the heroism of life.

But a chance also to see perhaps more than I wanted of the *fake* glamour, the pitiful parasitism of the West End of London.

And so I want you to let me stop . . . That will make it possible for me to leave England and see something of cleaner, fresher worlds than that which lies within the radius of a square mile of Piccadilly Circus . . . to do what I've always longed to do.

Now the column:

This is to say goodbye to you . . . it isn't a pleasant thing to do but I've got an opportunity that may never come my way again. Something I've wanted to do for a long time. Something that many of you who have written to me or come to see me have wanted to do yourselves. I'm going to see New York's Park Avenue, wander through the Bowery. I'm going to Mexico and listen to open-air opera in Hollywood's Bowl. I'm going to New Zealand, Australia, the South Seas. I'm making no settled plans. I shall wander as the spirit moves me.

There are some who will call me a fool for doing this. But I don't think youth should let the desire for security cramp the spirit of adventure. When you are young you should have the courage to seize the best out of life, so that when you are old you can think back on the years, and say: 'I have lived'. That is my philosophy of life.

I don't mind doing the unusual and when this leads to mistakes they at least teach me lessons which I do not forget. I am not ambitious. Or should I say that my ambition is only to do my utmost to taste the fullness of life? You who feel like me, who yearn to break away from the routine of your lives, will, I feel sure, understand the amount of determination one needs to do it. It's easy to talk of breaking away and leaving one's friends, but it is very hard to do so in practice. I'm lucky in that my family has so encouraged me. They are as enthusiastic as I am.

Meanwhile I want to thank you who, through my Personality Parade Fund, gave so many people pleasure, you whose Easter Egg gifts I was able to distribute to three thousand sick children.

Smile, perhaps, at its naivety, but the basic message remains today. Two messages in fact. One is that if one is sacked, as in my case, it can be a blessing in disguise. The other is that when one is young one *must* find a way to fulfil the adventures one dreams about . . . otherwise a sense of frustration remains for the rest of one's life, and one murmurs the two words 'if only'.

Yet, when I was young, it was so much easier to fulfil one's dreams, or try to do so, because one was not so harnessed by rules and regulations, and ridiculous psychological tests which determined whether one was suitable for this job or that. Bosses were independent. Appointment managers did not exist. Hence, if a boss interviewed someone for a job, he did not rely on the paperwork surrounding the applicant, he operated on instinct. 'He may not have the qualifications,' he might say, 'but I like him, and I *sense* he has the quality I'm looking for.'

That is what happened to me; and my mother's letter took me back to the moment when, without any academic qualifications, having failed at every examination at Harrow, I was lucky enough to obtain an introduction to Max Aitken, son of Lord Beaverbrook, later to become one of the heroes of the Royal Air Force. He talked, and listened, to me for half an hour, asked me for no academic qualifications ... then offered me a month's trial on the *Manchester Daily Express*. Would he have been able to give me such a chance today? Of course not. My application papers would never have reached him. I had not passed the intellectual test. Common sense, natural initiative, and intuition, do not belong to today's curriculum.

I went to Manchester and wrote in my diary on the first night, staying in a bed and breakfast in the famous Ackers Street of theatrical digs but now demolished, the line: 'This is the great chance of my life ... if I fail what on earth will happen to me?' I did not fail, and this was because from the moment I stepped through the entrance of the *Daily Express* office in Ancoats Street, I found myself among friends. There was no question of cold-shouldering a newcomer who had no qualifications to warrant him being there, no resentment that my presence was due to influence. Everyone rallied round to help me, sometimes rewriting a story I had written; and so there followed the happiest time I had up to then experienced in my life. My month's trial expired, but I had to wait another month before I was officially accepted as a full-

time reporter. And the acceptance followed an article I wrote called 'News After Dark', the first time
I ever saw my name in print. I had been given the
job of night reporter, on duty from eight at night
to four or five in the morning. Here is the article:

While you sleep I watch for news. A fire, a burglary, a murder ... the night reporter is there to
'cover' it.

A hospital attendant may tell me a badly injured
man has been brought in by ambulance. A policeman may tell me of a burglary. I investigate the
details and write the story, so that at whatever
hour it 'breaks' the news is on your breakfast table.
Streets are thronged with cinema goers when I
start. Cafés are filled with diners. Barmen are
pumping pints. In the office shorthand typists are
in telephone boxes taking 'copy'. Orders are being
flung around the newsroom. Sub-editors are building the paper. Until daybreak I watch for news in
Manchester and the surrounding districts.

Others are working. Bill is a night porter of a
hospital off Piccadilly. He has been there for ten
years and knows almost as much about the treatment of injuries as the doctors and nurses themselves.

Fred and Ted are night porters at another hospital. Fred used to be in the Lancashire regiment
and Ted in the Manchesters. Both served more
than seven years in India before they got their
present jobs. Fred once saw Gandhi in prison. It
was at Lahore. Fred was one of a party being
taken over the jail, and he saw what he describes
as a skeleton sitting in a cell. In that prison white

118

and coloured prisoners mix, and they occupy their time making oil cake for cattle.

For eighteen months Fred was stationed on the North West Frontier. He and his comrades used to be roused at night by the tribal snipers shooting on the tin roofs above their heads. Ted served for some time in the Andaman Islands in the Indian Ocean. It is a convict settlement where only those with life sentences are kept. The soldiers call it Gamblers' Paradise. There is nothing else to do. In India when a man gets a life sentence he is never allowed a remission. He may live on his own property and eventually his family is allowed to join him.

There is a nightwatchman I sometimes visit. His name is William Bromley. For twenty-nine years he has been guarding a steel works on the banks of the Manchester Ship Canal. His only companions are his dog Nellie and his revolver. He is proud of both. Nellie has been at his heels for twelve years, leaving him only to hunt for rats among the machinery. Her mother did the same for fourteen years. Bill says he has never had to shoot, but he always carries his revolver fully loaded, just in case. He has a permit for it.

Before the headquarters of the Salford Fire Brigade two arc lamps blaze on the War Memorial all night. The men are on duty in a building in the yard behind. Superintendent Stranaghan is their chief. He served in the Navy during the war. Chief Superintendent Sloan of the Manchester Fire Brigade was also a sailor. He served as an apprentice in a Shanghai–New York windjammer. He has the fireman's Victoria Cross, the King's Medal.

Thrills are plentiful. A policeman noticed a light flash through a window in offices in Market Street. He notified the police station, and five minutes later a dozen policemen arrived, surrounding the building. I watched them. They found a man hiding on the roof.

There was the dash across the moors after motor bandits. Two men had stolen a car in Liverpool after a smash-and-grab raid. They were reported to be making for Sheffield. Somewhere along the Snake Road a police car caught them and there was a smash. I reached the scene as the battered car of the bandits was being hauled away.

Tragedy is more intense in the early hours. A gas main blew up in an Oldham street. I was waiting in the hospital for news of the injured. I saw a woman sobbing in the waiting room. She was mother of a boy who had been gravely injured. He died next day. A few nights ago a pretty girl stood at the entrance of a Manchester Hospital. She was crying. I found she was a revue artist whose husband, the partner in her act, was so badly hurt in a street accident that his face may be scarred for life. Memories ... the little girl run over by a lorry, the sports car buckled against a telegraph pole with both occupants dead, the young man who had taken poison being carried twisting into the casualty ward.

Heavy lorries lumber through the streets, plain-clothes police officers walk in pairs. An occasional shop window brilliantly lit. Labourers shovelling grit on the cobbles. Taxicab drivers still hoping for fares.

Comes the dawn.

My mother's letter had set me on a journey into the past; and during the next few days I proceeded to look through my diaries of the times before I met Jeannie, before I went to Manchester. All the customary puzzlement, contradictions, insecurity, self-deception, were there in the diaries that belong to youth. One moment ever-confident, the next moment in despair. I found it entertaining sitting on the sofa in the cottage, Cherry on my lap, to read passages from the diaries that give clues to the way of life I have lived. Spasmodic passages:

I do not look back upon my Harrow School days with pleasure. I was looking for a Svengali, a master who would guide me in the labyrinth of growing up. My housemaster should have been the one, but he was vacuous. I once missed a catch in an important inter-house cricket match, and afterwards he hauled me up and said I was useless to society. And the only advice I ever received from him was that I must never be rude to other people's servants. Amazing!

I was a failure. I didn't pass any examinations, and although I had my moments of success, being made captain both of cricket and football of the junior house teams, I faded out after that. No sporting achievements. Yet I can look back upon that as a bit of luck.

Those who are successful at school go on to the real life with a disadvantage. They think life is going to be easy. Failure like mine is better for my character. I'm better prepared to meet the shocks and buffets of the world than a boy who has carried

the honours at his school. That is an optimistic
way of regarding my failures . . . but it is also true
that a boy who fails acquires the seeds of an inferiority complex. I know. I have those seeds. Why
was I a failure? I believe I was too hasty. I took
just a little too much for granted. I expected success without effort, without doing the spadework
first. But there were gains from my Harrow schooldays. I admit that. I learnt, for instance, that life is
very often unfair, and that one must overcome this
feeling of unfairness. Why should a boy be beaten
because he slipped on a loose carpet, dropping the
tray of eggs and bacon he was taking to a prefect's
breakfast party? Or because he didn't clean the
shoes to a prefect's satisfaction? Or because he was
caught having a pillow fight with a fellow member
of the dormitory after lights out? All very unfair,
but such incidents are a preview of the troubles
that lie ahead in life. That was Harrow's best gift
to me.

I have my first job. I'm a typist in Lever Brothers,
an office boy really because I'm at the beck and
call of clerks in a department named GCA/UEL/
MED. Someone calls out: 'Tea, Tangye,' and I
scurry off and fetch a cup.

I've been six months now at Lever Brothers and
I'm not getting anywhere. True I've had a rise of
five shillings a week but the work hasn't any respon-
sibility. Outside in the deb world I'm having quite
a lot of fun, though I always feel doubtful about
myself. I don't feel confident when I meet people.
Last week I decided to pick up again my idea of

enrolling in a journalist course. Oh dear, that last time when I was at Harrow, and I read the lessons at the bottom of my bed by torchlight! And then Gordon Meggy, the director of the course, found out I was a schoolboy, and advised me to concentrate on my school lessons. But he had started me off and I will always remember his helpfulness. This time I've been in touch with Sir Max Pemberton who is head of the London School of Journalism, and I sent him a sample of what I've written. And he's written back a personal letter urging me to go on writing. But I can't possibly afford the fee.

Over two months since I've written my diary. I'm as lazy as ever, and I far prefer to look into space than to write an article or short story which is certain to be returned.

Had a fortnight down in Cornwall, and I have become a besotted admirer of Marcel Proust. 'Swann's Way' is the first part of his novel *Remembrance of Things Past*, and it is for me a sensational beginning. I find dazzling wisdom and comfort in his writings, and answers to subconscious questions that I so often search for and fail to find. He describes feelings that I have but which I have never been able to pin down, and his description of a man in love reflects my own innermost feelings. What is more, his habit of inquiring into his own thoughts encourages me to do the same. I believe that at last I have found someone to guide me in life.

Slowly but surely I'm conquering my laziness, but what else am I doing? My mind is full of opposites. I know one thing but do another. I seem to be fighting against myself, a sort of civil war within myself. I never seem able to form concrete views on anything. I seem unable to break out. My true self is imprisoned within me. My mind cannot assemble my inner arguments and I remain in a state of confusion. I figure out that my mind is developing at a very late period. It is trying to make up time for that it lost at school. I am an idealist but I cannot put my finger on my ideals.

About my career. In my heart of hearts I want to write. But I am frightened. How on earth do I earn enough money to enable me to do so? I'm doing a Short Story Course now but it is leading me nowhere. And what experience of life have I had which would enable me to write anything worthwhile? I just don't know what to do. Perhaps destiny will make a choice for me.

Destiny has done so! I was interviewed by two directors of the Lever Brothers subsidiary Joseph Crosfields and Sons, and yesterday I was told I had been chosen for a travelling salesman's job in Warrington selling soap, and it would be for two years and I would have to leave by the 8.30 a.m. train on Monday morning! The salary was £175 a year plus hotel expenses. Just think of all those among the two million unemployed who would have jumped at the chance, but I have refused! I had no doubt about doing so. The feeling in me was so powerful that it was as if a kind of spiritual force was driving me. I will have to leave Lever Brothers, that is certain. They won't think kindly of someone who turns down such a chance. But I will be *free*! Working in that office has been suffocating my mind, and I sense in a most extraordinary way that I'll look back on this moment, and realize it is the turning point in my life.

VIII

The summer was ending. The swallows, companions since May, were sweeping in and out of the garage which is really an open barn, giving the impression of frantic excitement; and that is always a signal that the long voyage to South Africa is stirring within them; and I felt sad, thinking of the hazards ahead of them. I had wanted to make life easy for them when they arrived in May, fixing a special ledge to make their nest-building easy. They preferred to make their own mudcaked nest against a beam instead. But they had no hazards at Minack, unlike the swallows a visitor told me about. 'My neighbour,' the lady said, 'takes a broom when the swallows have made their nests, and knocks them down. She says she doesn't want the walls of her house dirtied.'

The General had lost the gleam of his spring and early summer feathers. He looked tarnished as he hobbled up to the escallonia restaurant. It was his left leg which made him limp. I cannot say what made him do so. He may have landed heavily. Perhaps he had a gun pellet lodged in his body. Whatever it was, it made him hobble.

Merlin and Susie remained happy because there continued to be an array of callers at the Solitude gate to flatter them, callers who if they were wise, and they were mostly wise, would lean over the gate, offering presents . . . carrots, tea biscuits. And if they were wiser still, they would keep some of the presents out of view until they had climbed over the stile into Oliver land, intending perhaps a stroll to the Ambrose rock; then, by suddenly revealing the remaining presents, the callers would find to their joy they had succeeded in bribing Merlin and Susie to be their guides.

This joy, however, could sometimes prove to be a dubious pleasure. These self-appointed guides had firm ideas as to how to guide. Hence a couple might set off up the field towards the gap which leads to the blackthorn alley and experience a barrage of donkey head-pushing in their backs; and the reason would be that the couple had exhausted their presents, a situation that Merlin and Susie did not appreciate.

One turns right at the gap into the blackthorn alley, and thereupon a further hazard can develop. The blackthorn alley is narrow, edged in on either side by blackthorn, unruly brambles, and, in late summer, a profusion of sloes. Indeed the blackthorn alley troubles my conscience at summer's end. Jeannie and I used to go there on a lovely still morning picking blackberries, or sloes; Jeannie used to brew sloe gin, and to this day I have bottles which she brewed and which, for sentimental reasons, I have never touched. Fred and Penny were

our helpers in those days; and there was always a
competition as to whether their large mouths gob-
bled the blackberries before we got them first. My
conscience is troubled that I no longer have the
time to pick the blackberries and the sloes. Nor the
wish, perhaps.

The hazard of the blackthorn alley, however, is
that its narrowness provides an excellent opportunity for the guides to display their individuality.
Sometimes, for instance, they hang back, munching at whatever they fancy; and then suddenly
decide that, in the role of guides, they should be in
front of those they are guiding. Thus they will
charge at those ahead of them, treating them as if
they are ghosts, knocking them aside. The consequences can be tricky. There has never been a
serious complaint, but there have been one or two
people who, after setting off happily, have come
back to tell me, humorously, that Merlin and Susie
seemed to be eccentric guides. There is no vice in
the characters of Merlin and Susie, no donkeys
could be more gentle, but one must be on guard
against a sudden irritation on their part. A horsefly
might nip them, and a hind leg might fling out as a
consequence. Trusting children may be at risk in
such circumstances. I leave it to the common sense
of the parents to watch their children.

Children . . . It is one of the saddest events of
the late twentieth century that children have
become victims of media exploitation. I know how
this started because of the experience Jeannie and
I had in the journalistic world. At half past four

every afternoon, one can imagine a meeting of newspaper executives or television executives. They are concerned about the news stories and the television programmes of the following twenty-four hours. There is no obvious news. The world, for the moment, seems to be placid. Despair on the part of the executives. What can we do? And the answer is, we must make some news. In this way a media campaign will begin. Some small item will be magnified into a huge issue. Easily done. Get a few people of prominence to give their views, in favour or against the item at issue, and there can be a torrent of news excitement for a few days; and then another item takes its place.

The item, however, which began with the ill-treatment of a child, has spawned an issue which is affecting all our lives, children and grown-ups alike. The issue is child abuse. The evil of genuine child abuse is a matter for the courts, but there has developed a grey area of alleged child abuse; and within this area a campaign has been nurtured in which children are led to believe that any sign of affection, or of attention, by an adult, has some form of connection with the child abuse syndrome they are told about. The Biblical phrase, 'Suffer the little children to come unto me,' has now become a phrase of threat. Instead of behaving naturally with a child, one must be on guard. Thanks to the hype surrounding the campaign, a child misinterpreting genuine affection, or, as in other cases, creating mischief, can use the free telephone service to report an incident that has no justification to be reported; and this results in a police investigation when no police investigation is warranted, and in great unnecessary distress being caused. For an example, a young mother was asked by her little daughter to share her bed. Does that mean, the young mother asked me, that I am guilty of child abuse?

One is inclined to accept campaigns by pressure groups without thinking what they signify. Anything more silly, for instance, than a lady in an office going to court to sue a gentleman colleague for 'sexual harassment' . . . when all he was doing was paying her the compliment of flirting with her? Who are these strange but articulate, powerful people who succeed in having laws passed to stop us having pleasure? . . . and it is the pleasure of being natural with children that the child abuse campaigners are destroying.

It was September now, and it was a September evening when I first began to learn the facts about Jeannie's illness. The doctor had come and I had remained outside sitting on the white seat. Jeannie came out of the cottage, dusk falling and, when passing me, just said she was going to pick some tomatoes to give the doctor. Then the doctor came out and joined me on the white seat, and told me what he feared. How should one react on such an occasion? Say, 'Thank you very much for letting me know,' as if he were giving a weather forecast? Or react as I did, as I sat on the white seat which had begun its life in Jeannie's St Albans home, Bryher Lodge, Avenue Road, by exclaiming: 'Impossible! It couldn't happen to her, couldn't happen!'

September . . . daddy long legs prevailed, appearing in unwelcome places, testing one's patience, provoking a wicked inclination to smash them, an inclination which is restrained by a warning note within one . . . never kill a unit of Creation unless it is a question of self-preservation. There are spiders in the bath, and one wonders why, having travelled up the waste pipe, the pipe hole still open, they do not return the way they came, instead of trying to climb up the walls of the bath, too steep, too smooth for them successfully to do so; and there follows the effort of collecting them gently in a handkerchief or a towel before the hot tap is turned on.

End of September time, and there were apples still to pick, to peel, to stew, pears too. It is a time when bracken is losing its sheen, and becoming dark and ragged. A time when one walks along spider-web-covered paths, or is standing still, and is arrested by a few notes of a robin's autumn song, then silence, as if its purpose was to bewail the now long-ago spring and summer. People called.

A young couple. 'We are on honeymoon,' said the man. 'We were married three days ago, and my wife insisted that our honeymoon should be at Lamorna, so that we could come to Minack.' The young wife, deliciously pretty, had been in the musical *Cats* in London.

A middle-aged man arrived, and I listened to him as he sat in the porch.

'My wife died three years ago,' he said, 'and I went to pieces. One evening I was in my chair in our home when I looked up and saw my wife ... clearly, absolutely clearly, standing there in front of me, and she spoke to me in the voice I knew so well. "Pull yourself together," she said. "You've got a future, find someone else. I only want you to be happy."

'It was all so vivid. I, a cynic, was convinced.'

A young girl arrived with her family. She was a violinist in the Southampton Youth Orchestra, recently back from a short tour of America. I told her how I loved hearing a violin being played in the open air, in a wild place, where the countryside served as the audience.

A few months later she returned ... with her violin. She went up to the bridge and began playing. I did not watch her. I hid out of sight, a member of the countryside audience, listening to *Ave Maria*.

A woman called, and I asked her to come in, but she stood still, holding up a photograph of a girl.

'Yes?' I questioned.

'It is a photograph of my daughter,' she replied, 'and back in the winter she made plans to come here to see you this week, this very day, and I am representing her.'

'Yes?'

'She was killed in a motor accident five weeks ago.'

Some people exclaim that life is funny. I have never felt that way, because sadness seems always to be around the corner. I suppose their intention is to avoid reality. Media moguls encourage them. The television screen is filled with endless unreal comedies punctured, every few seconds, by artificial laughter. Such comedies, obviously, are a merry way of taking minds away from personal troubles, but I wish there was a balance. I wish there was more subtlety. I wish there were more opportunities to feel, as one does after listening to a great orchestra playing a tumultuous symphony, an elation. One listens, and the soul is stirred. There is little soul-stirring created by the media producers of today.

September . . . soon holidaymakers will be back in their homes, soon the warblers, the flycatchers, the swallows, the martins will have left the countryside, badgers will be refurbishing their setts, foxes will be looking for mates, hunting will have begun, pheasants and grouse will be shot, spent cartridges will fall to the ground.

It is a time when I suffer from a sense of lassitude, and I have to summon a tenacity from within me. Perhaps for the past months I have been assembling notes, the pleasantest period of writing a book. There is no deadline to threaten, no fear that an interruption will interfere with one's line of thought, no mental effort required. The mind is idle when suddenly one has an idea, and one jots it down on any piece of paper one can find. Something achieved . . . and I go back to contemplation.

My way of controlling my notes is to keep a foolscap notebook, on the left side of which I copy out any haphazard notes of descriptions I have made, any quotations from books and what people say to me, philosophical comments of my own, and current matters which stir me. On the right-hand side of the notebook, I try to list the incidents around which the book I have in mind will be written. When I have marked out one hundred such incidents, I feel I have a book to write. At this point I must summon the tenacity to start writing, and continue to write despite interruptions. I put a blank piece of paper into the typewriter, head it 'Chapter One', and just stare at it. A lonely moment.

Jeannie would look after the details of life while I was writing, just as I used to look after the details when she was writing. I would not have to move from Minack territory. She would greet visitors, do the shopping, provide a supper while I was still at work, feed the little birds, feed the gulls, feed a cat. She protected me and, because she had such a scintillating mind, inspired me.

These responsibilities were now mine, and it required tenacity on my part to deal with them. I was so tempted, time and again, to let things go. The tenacity within me, however, stopped me.

In summertime Merlin and Susie cause little trouble. There is grass galore for them to eat, and succulent brambles and honeysuckle ... and my main task is to keep them supplied with drinking water. The trough, in which the water is stored, is an unusual one. We first had it during the war years in our Mortlake cottage; its purpose at that time was the storing of fresh eggs. It is only about two feet square and three feet deep, and it has a special design which is of special earthenware material. Around its top is a ridge which had to be kept filled with water, acting as a cooler, a Heath Robinson kind of refrigerator. We kept other things in it as well as fresh eggs, but the fresh eggs are what I mainly remember. The ration at the time was two eggs a week per person, but at the bottom of the garden Jeannie and I kept half a dozen Rhode Island Reds whose home was the cement-built air-raid shelter; and at a flush time of laying, we used to store the eggs in this earthenware contraption which is now the drinking trough of the donkeys.

In winter time, however, they test my tenacity every late afternoon. They expect my attention around half past four, and if I do not appear Susie will bellow a hee-haw. I am their private butler who is expected to bring their evening meal on time. They live, for the most part, on Oliver land and they have a wood home there, built to withstand the Cornish storms by a father-and-son team called Hepworth, which I paid for out of money left by Jeannie when she died. Thus it is called Jeannie's shelter. One half is for the donkeys, the other half for the Leyland tractor and the Condor, and the storage of hay and straw.

I have, however, to walk up the lane, across Monty's Leap and beyond, to reach the Solitude gate which opens into Oliver land. Such a walk is pleasant enough on normal occasions, on pleasant afternoons when the weather is calm, but I develop a battle with tenacity when there is a howling gale and cascading rain waiting to accompany me on my butler role. 'I don't think it's *really* necessary to feed them,' I murmur to myself as I sit in front of the log fire. 'Surely they can do without me for one evening.' But my tenacity conquers. I suddenly leap from my chair, put on my mac and march out into the wind and the rain, a packet of biscuits in my hand.

I walk down the lane and across Monty's Leap, scaring a blackbird from the hydrangea where it had decided to settle for the night; and all the while the rain is lashing my face, freezing my hands, and tearing across the countryside, omnipotent, laughing in the knowledge that no computer can control it.

I reach the Solitude gate, and there are Merlin and Susie waiting for me, two bedraggled donkeys who whimper at the sight of me, pushing their heads to the top of the gate, impatient for me to open the packet of biscuits they knew I would be bringing. 'Patience,' I call out, 'patience!' And their patience is required as I struggle, as always, to scratch the wrapper open with my fingers.

My butler role, however, is by no means complete. I give them three biscuits each to keep them quiet, then I gingerly climb over the stile beside the gate. Carter's stile, I call it, because it was created by a freelance gardener who once helped me, and who said one day, 'I've worked in gardens all over Cornwall all my life, but all my work has been anonymous, nothing achieved to make me feel I will be remembered.' It was then that I said, 'We can put that right. This stile will always be known as Carter's stile.'

I was in the field on one such occasion and I turned left, walking the few yards to the back of the shelter, undoing the latch which was kept in place by a knot of string, then opening the double door, and finding a moment of peace from the wind and the rain. No peace from the donkeys, though. They had followed me, and it was now my job to keep them at bay while I collected an armful of hay. I still had some remaining biscuits and they knew it; and so it was now a situation where they nudged me, pushed me, as I carried the hay outside, and round to the door, a door which I always kept half open, which opened into the private sanctuary of Merlin and Susie. I reached it safely, spread the hay in a clean corner, and proceeded to sit on a seat, in the form of concrete blocks, to watch the donkeys eat; and to listen to them munch. A munch, the sound of which is therapeutic.

Here was a time for wandering contemplation, the donkeys munching, the wind howling, the rain ricocheting against the window, and my conscience clear. My tenacity had conquered my laziness. I had left the warmth of the cottage. I had fed the donkeys.

A previous tenant of Minack but who lived in the farm of Rosemodres up the lane, was called Trewern. He was blind, and he had a carthorse, a favourite grey and white carthorse, which he stabled in the stable at Minack. He used to come down the lane, unassisted, then go into the stable, and sit there, listening, as it was described to Jeannie and me, 'to the shuffle of the horse's hooves on the cobbles'. We were told that story when we first came, and it had charmed us both. Evidence, we thought, of tranquillity. And now here I was on another seat, a concrete seat, on the other side of the valley to where Trewern sat, experiencing a similar tranquillity. Donkeys munching, a gale blowing, rain lashing.

I sat there musing, my bird brain jumping from subject to subject. I found myself thinking of the hypocrisy that had denied a public lottery but permitted football pools. I have been a consistent football pool enthusiast and so was Jeannie. There was the occasion when our dear friend Sir Alan Herbert – known nationally as A. P. H., wit, one-time Member of Parliament for Oxford University, playwright of such musicals as *Bless the Bride*, *bon viveur*, author of *Misleading Cases* which had a television series long before *Rumpole*, a fervent football pool enthusiast who wrote a comical book called *Pools Pilot* – died and his memorial service was held at St Martin-in-the-Fields. Jeannie and I were determined to attend, but money was short. 'Alan!' Jeannie called out the week before, looking up into the heavens. 'Use your influence and all your football knowledge.' And seemingly he did. That week we won £98 on the pools.

I, not long ago, was even more fortunate. I pay my pool investment six months in advance. I have a static choice of numbers in the treble chance pool. No attempt by me to nominate clubs. Nor do I have to check the results because Littlewoods do this for me. I am engaged in a lottery therefore. Week after week, month after month, I hear no news of a win. None the less at the back of my mind there is always a hope of a win . . . and not long ago it *happened*. And in this way.

I have a dislike of opening buff envelopes. I suppose this may be because buff envelopes are usually the bearers of unwelcome bills. Then there came a day, it was a Friday, when a buff envelope arrived in the morning post. One glance and I threw it aside. A couple of days later I was once again aiming to clean up my desk when I picked up the discarded envelope, and opened it. I shrieked! Inside was a cheque for £1200, and a polite note from Littlewoods wishing me greater success in the future.

I sat there on my cement seat when Merlin moved away from the hay he had been munching, coming up to me, pushing his nose at my tummy. I remembered the biscuits which I still had in my pocket. Merlin had remembered . . . and so I stopped my musing and gave him three biscuits, then another three, and by then Susie had joined in, and the packet was emptied.

My bird brain went off on another tack. Such a different tack. I sat there thinking about love affairs. Those of people I have known. I have watched them blossom, been maintained for a while then fade away, as one or the other decide to take up again the routine of their lives. Those wild intoxicating moments, captured in photographs and letters, vibrant at the time, turn to shadows. How lucky I was with Jeannie! Then my bird brain switched to the perennial question: 'How does one know when one is in love?' There is an answer which may be too simple for some, may be too simple to be true. It is to ask oneself: 'To whom would you want to tell first of any incident concerning yourself, and be excited at the thought of doing so?'

My bird brain now returned to Jeannie, and the letter the young astrologer had sent to me. How strange it was that his wife had seen her so clearly. How strange that Jeannie had chosen her to send the message to me . . . 'Jeannie said she's spending also a lot of time with you around her old haunts. Time and space are different to her now. She's shown you she's around still, and will do so again soon.'

It was the last five words which suddenly hit me . . . 'and will do so again soon.'

I realized it was a week after the letter had arrived that Garry Boon, producer of the *Songs of Praise* programme, invited me to appear in it. The Minack part was filmed in early October, and the programme shown on BBC1 at the end of October. It had been, as I have already said, a happy two days' filming. Pam Rhodes, the interviewer, was so natural and feminine that it was effortless to talk to her. The cameraman Ian Stacey was so patient and encouraging, and the sound man Peter Rose displayed great patience as a trainer helicopter from the Culdrose Naval Station droned overhead, stopping any progress in the filming. There I was sitting on the concrete seat, listening to the donkeys munching, the rain lashing, the gale roaring, when I suddenly knew that Jeannie *had* reached me.

For when *Songs of Praise* was shown, there was a lovely shot of Cherry with me in the porch, a talk with me, a vision of the donkeys ... and then an inside shot of the inside of the cottage.

Suddenly, out of nowhere, there was Jeannie. First the legendary photograph of her by Baron, the camera lingering. Then a minute or two later, the beautiful portrait of her by Kanelba, the Polish painter; and again the camera lingered.

It was as if she was with me at Minack again.

IX

I like November. Everything is at rest, recovering from the ebullience of summer and autumn. One is living in suspense, and I find myself able to concentrate: making decisions, making notes of what has to be done in the months ahead. The garden must be dug over, the sides of the lane cut down, and the daffodil meadows mowed with the Condor. I am lucky in that I have a friend, Steve, who will do these heavy tasks for me. This dark, sturdy Cornishman will come to me on a Saturday when I need him. He has an enthusiasm with which he will tackle any job as if it was a bonus for him to have the chance to do so. He lifts my morale. He will give me earthy advice as to whether I should do this or that. He will arrive from Camborne at eight o'clock in the morning, and work like a hurricane till three or four; and then instead of going immediately home, he will go wandering around the fields and the cliff. He loves Minack.

He urged me one day to have the elms sawn down, and said that he would arrange it, and there would be no problems. The elms had been standing looking naked ever since the elm disease attacked and killed them. They looked very unsightly, but I had always kept postponing taking any action. Yes, it was time they were sawn down, and Steve declared that he and a friend of his would do so.

The elms, in their heyday, circled elegantly around a meadow close to the cottage where we used to grow Governor Herrick violets, called the Gertie meadow after the legendary actress Gertrude Lawrence. Gertie was a long-time friend, and she once chose me to write her biography. Her lawyers sent me a handsome contract including free expenses for travel to New York, Hollywood and elsewhere, but I refused. Jeannie and I had just arrived at Minack and nothing was going to budge us. Gertie was touched by our determination, and she thereupon asked us to name a meadow after her so that, she said, there would always be a corner of England which would be a memorial to her. We chose the violet meadow. Hence it was Gertie's meadow around which circled the elm trees.

I used to look at the decayed trees and remember a play called *The Petrified Forest* by Robert Sherwood, which was turned into a movie starring Humphrey Bogart, Leslie Howard and Bette Davis. The movie has haunted me at intervals all my life, always will, because of four lines spoken by Leslie Howard from a poem by the French poet François Villon . . . just four lines which made an indelible impression upon me. Unfortunately the impression was emotional not factual, and I have never been able to remember them. They served as the theme of *The Petrified Forest*, but from the moment I was first dazzled by them they went out of my mind. Just the emotion remained.

But soon after seeing the movie, I had the opportunity to capture again the words which had so moved me because I was asked by my editor to interview Bette Davis.

She was staying in a Park Lane hotel, and I interviewed her, sharing a hard settee in the foyer. She had broken her arm, which was in a sling. I am vague now as to the questions I asked her because my mind was full of the one and only question I needed personally to be answered. Hell to the interview. I didn't care if the editor lambasted me for bringing back nothing. All I wanted to know were those four lines in *The Petrified Forest* that were quoted from the works of François Villon.

And she obliged.

She spoke them to me as I sat entranced, sitting beside her on the hard settee, so entranced that I forgot them immediately; and to this day I have forgotten them. Only the emotion remained as I looked at the petrified forest around Gertie's meadow.

November is, of course, a nostalgic month for many. Owen, a soldier of the D-Day campaign, knocked at the porch door with a tray of poppies.

'Armistice Day coming up again,' he said apologetically.

I gave him a donation and in return he gave me a poppy. Then he said, as if my donation merited a bonus, 'Here's a special one for the car.'

I held both poppy and bonus in my hand.

'Do you find that people of today know what this is all about?' I asked.

'The real people do,' he replied, 'but there are not many of them. The rest think it's a waste of time and money. They do not know as we know that the young people of those times died for freedom.'

'And those who have died since,' I added.

Television has made violence so impersonal. Viewers sit in front of their sets, munching fast food, gulping a glass of wine, observing dispassionately the bombardment of Dubrovnik, for instance, watching a marvellously self-controlled television reporter, male or female, staring briefly into the camera, speaking their lines, calmly describing the horrors in the neighbourhood. What for? Just to entertain us. The television coverage of the Gulf War was the ultimate in detached horror reporting. This was a soap opera. What fun! We could listen to the words of a reporter aboard an aircraft which despatched a missile, and listen to another reporter in Baghdad describing its arrival. No humanitarian reasons for such exposure. Just a way of boosting television ratings.

The mood was different in the Hitler war. There was no hint of it being a soap opera. Those who were involved believed in the cause they were fighting for and, although the press probed, there was no theatrical display of probing. There was instead this belief, so powerful that it cannot be rationally explained in today's language, that to die in battle was to enhance the lives of those who would follow them. How old-fashioned this sounds.

At the time, because those who were dying belonged to my generation, I found myself specially aware of the sacrifice they were altruistically making; and I conceived the idea of a book which contained tributes to those who had been killed, including air-raid victims; and each tribute written by a personal friend of the one who had been killed. It was before Pearl Harbor, before the United States came into the war. Britain was standing alone against Hitler. The odds against survival seemed logically impossible. Yet there was this spiritual power to do so.

> Went the day well?
> We died and never knew,
> But, well or ill, England,
> We died for you.

I called the collection of tributes for the book *Went the Day Well*. Several distinguished writers of the time contributed, and there were some who were unknown, and for whom I 'ghosted' their story. It was during this period that Jeannie and I began to develop that sense of companionship, that chemical relationship, which is the essence of a love affair. We would, in our spare time, go off to see people who had known a special friend who had been killed. I found myself emotionally affected by the reactions of those we saw, but what I remember most clearly was the sensitivity of

Jeannie. She was so natural in her sympathy. There was no need for her to be taught how to understand. Instinct guided her. She did not need rules to follow. She did not need training. I watched her, watched her integrity; and fell in love with her.

The royalties earned from *Went the Day Well* were paid to the Red Cross Prisoners of War Fund in the first instance; and when after the war, during the sixties, it was reprinted, the royalties were paid to the Star and Garter Home at Richmond.

Recently I have re-read the letter Mr Churchill wrote to me from Downing Street on 27 April 1942:

> It was very good of you to think of sending me a special copy of *Went the Day Well*, which you have edited.
>
> I have had an opportunity during the Easter weekend to look through part of the book, and am very much obliged to you for it.
>
> Winston Churchill.

That evening when Owen, carrying his tray of poppies, said apologetically, 'Armistice Day coming up again,' I sat in the cottage and my mind roamed back to the moment when, living in Cholmondely House overlooking the river at Richmond, I had the idea for *Went the Day Well*: and began to write, in front of a November log fire, first the prologue:

This is the story of men and women who bade goodbye to their days of peace to die for gains they will never share. They came from many different lands, spoke many different tongues, yet all of them gave their lives for the same beliefs.

They did not want to die. For dying meant leaving good friends, happy homes, and clear blue skies, and the salt of the sea, and rounds of golf, and walks across the moors, and drinks at the club, and the wind at night, and the scent of log fires. For dying meant they never would know whether or not they had fought in vain.

Yet when the moment of cold decision ended the brightness of their lives their thoughts did not halt them; and they died so that their beliefs might live.

Some may call them heroes, but they themselves would not wish to be considered such; because each, according to his fashion, did his duty ... expecting neither reward nor recognition ...

They are of the cavalcade of freedom. Labourers and clerks, playboys and housewives, students and old men, typists and nurses; all these and many more who march the road of danger and sacrifice so that the lights of cities may blaze again, and the lands be filled with song ...

And so it was ... that I thought of the story of this book. A story not to be written by a single person, but by a company of people each of whom had known the savagery of personal loss. A story that would tell how men and women of this age lived full lives and met sudden deaths. How they gloried in doing their duty and how they paved the way for life to become normal again. How courage was their companion and tenacity their sword . . .

Men and women who, through the centuries to come, will always be remembered.

This is the story . . .

and then the epilogue:

. . . That is the story. If, having read it, we have a feeling of grimness it will not have been told in vain. For if out of the pages there stepped a ghost he might tell us there are some who forget, who forget the dead who died for them, who forget the blind who were blinded for them, who forget the maimed who were maimed for them.

He might ask us to close our eyes sometimes and vision the last moments of some who have gone . . . the airman who in a spiral dive struggles in vain to free himself from the cockpit; the bomber crew whose plane is ablaze; the seaman who lingers in icy water; the soldier who chokes blood in the desert; the patriot who stands against a wall in the dawn with a handkerchief around his eyes.

He might ask us to think sometimes about these men and women; about the anguish in their hearts and the twisting pain in their bodies; about the loved ones they left behind and about the children they will never see grow old.

He might ask, then, to swear vengeance; vengeance not only against the enemy, but against the old world which preferred them to die young. He might ask us to show our vengeance, not in our bitterness, but in our defiance of the hell still to come; in our ruthless resolution to win the peace that will come too.

For out of the peace, out of the great new world those who are left will build, these men and women will find their memorial.

As I read again those lines it was evening, and I had just come back from feeding the donkeys, in Oliver land, the land with a view overlooking Mount's Bay, the best view any donkey could have. A southerly gale was blowing, white horses racing in a grey sea, a river of the dying light in the sky to the west, a buzzard hovering, the horizon as a backdrop, salt in the air; the donkeys standing at the Solitude gate, expecting more apples which I didn't have: Cherry waiting for me on my return to the cottage, a shadow beside the white seat; the General, having had his peanut supper, ready to limp off to his night hideout, but vexed by the sight of me coming up the path and blocking his way; and up there on the roof was the evening gull.

I sat there ruminating about the last line of the epilogue, 'these men and women will find their memorial.'

How does that memorial stand today?

The material advantages gained are too obvious to list. Yet what is the price? Unemployment is one price. The cleverer the machines, the more they will take away work from the people. This is common sense. No industrialist is going to employ fifty men when he can invest in a machine that does their work at the push of a button. Unemployment is here to stay. That is one high price to be paid for the material advantages gained.

How else does that memorial stand?

When those in the book set out to serve in the Hitler war there was no fear about going for a stroll after dark. There was no thought that old women would be battered by burglars in their homes. Front doors were left unlocked, security advisers did not exist, police were not knifed and shot at, fear did not rule the cities. There was a wonderful naturalness of trust when those men and women set out for the Hitler war.

They believed, for instance, in loyalty, and today loyalty is a dirty word. Loyalty would mean loyalty to the firm they worked for. They had the confidence that they would spend their life with the firm concerned, sharing its progress and its setbacks, relying on the firm's loyalty in return; and earning a gold watch at the end of their time. Very dull this may sound, but it provided the cloak of security which offered normality in the everyday life of those concerned. Not any more. City columns of the press toss around the names of this firm or that which may be about to be taken over, and so destroy the destinies of those whose contentment revolved around security ... and who suddenly find themselves redundant. All this done under the umbrella of increasing so-called efficiency.

What is gained? I am puzzled as to what is gained in terms of happiness. I am puzzled by the way brilliant minds, accountants, lawyers, politicians, possessors of all the fashionable university degrees, perpetually attending conferences, elaborating their contradictory theories on television, are incapable of cooperating with each other. I am puzzled by the way the Prime Minister and the Leader of the Opposition shout at each other, like unruly schoolboys, in the House of Commons for all the world to see. I am puzzled by the way the brutal fact is ignored that the press-button machine age has taken over, and permanent unemployment is the inevitable outcome. Science has conquered humanity.

How else does that memorial stand?

Those men and women set off for the Hitler war inspired by their passion to defend their homes, their streets, their way of life, from the Hitler enemy, then later from a threatening Soviet enemy. What has happened to many of those homes, those streets today?

Then there is the gradual destruction of individual freedom. Freedom is a passport to take risks, to make one's own decisions, right ones or wrong ones, without being hamstrung by a multitude of petty regulations devised by faceless members of committees. There were enough such petty regulations before the advent of the Common Market, but now the faceless members of European committees are bombarding us with petty-regulations of *Alice in Wonderland* proportions; and in order to keep their jobs they will keep up the momentum by more and more such regulations. What is their long-term purpose? Is their aim to create a police state by the back door? A prison in which we are all dutiful prisoners?

And all the while the lessons of history, and recent history, are being ignored. The British Empire disintegrated because its members no longer wanted to be controlled by London; the Soviet Union revolted against being controlled by Moscow; and Scotland wants to be divorced from Westminster. Isn't it obvious that history will be repeated and that, in due course, once people have fully realized that they have surrendered their freedom to intellectual theorists, there will be a revolt against being controlled by Brussels?

The theorists who dominate the faceless committees have never learnt the lesson that, in the end, the heart, the passion of the people, will always defeat those who theorize. It was the heart which sent the men and women of *Went the Day Well* into battle, thus saving Britain from the Nazi domination to which the rest of Europe had already surrendered ... an everlasting example of how the heart of the United Kingdom defeated the theorists who argued that victory on our own was impossible.

I had an unhappy experience concerning *Went the Day Well*; and I am still haunted by it. The book made a dramatic impression on the public; and the BBC Overseas Service kept broadcasting extracts to the occupied territories. One of the contributors to the book was Sir Michael Balcon, powerful head of the then Ealing Studios. I invited him to contribute an appreciation of his godson

Pen Tennyson, a promising film director who had married Nora Pilbeam, a young film star of that time. Pen Tennyson was killed in a flying accident; and when in due course Michael Balcon sent me his appreciation of his godson, I was very touched by its charm and sincerity.

Not long after *Went the Day Well* was published, I had a letter from Ealing Studios, saying that Sir Michael had completed a film which he intended to call *Went the Day Well*, thus cashing in on the publicity that the genuine *Went the Day Well* was receiving. There is no copyright in titles. I was at his mercy. There was nothing I could do to stop the title being used.

'Only if you can appeal to Sir Michael's good taste,' advised my lawyer, 'can you stop it.'

I failed. The film has been repeatedly shown over the years by the BBC. The title blazoned, the quotation, which I had found in the guestbook of a house near Woodstock in Oxfordshire, staring into the viewer's face; and no acknowledgement given whence the title and the quotation came.

> Went the day well?
> We died and never knew,
> Well or ill, Freedom,
> We died for you.

Jeannie and I never saw the film when it was shown in London. We were never aware of what had happened until years later when at last we had a television at Minack and one evening we turned it on, and found how that beautiful title had been exploited. I remember the cry of Jeannie. 'What a cheat!'

What also upset us profoundly was that Michael Balcon had written to us at Minack, asking us if we could find copies of the now out-of-print *Went the Day Well*. In all innocence we tried to help him.

The other day I read through the file dealing with the creation of *Went the Day Well*. There were several interesting letters, and there was a particular one from the remarkable Lady MacRobert. When she lost her third, and youngest RAF son, she wrote the following to the Secretary of State for Air:

> It is my wish to make a mother's immediate reply, in the way that I know would be my boys' reply . . . attacking, striking sharply, straight to the mark . . . the gift of £25,000 towards the cost of a bomber to carry on their work in the most effective way. This expresses my reaction on receiving the news about my sons.

After reading the letter in the press I wrote to her, asking if she would like to write a tribute to her sons, and I received this reply:

> Thanks for yours of the 9th inst with its interesting suggestion. Such a book as you describe should be of great benefit to all, and show up the wonderful heroism of our Youth of Britain and the Empire, and I feel very pleased that you should include 'my boys' in those representing such a sacrifice,

and would be quite willing to write such a tribute ... the lines you quote, however, in *my* opinion are inadequate, as they died for more than England.

The last sentence sunk into my mind. I thereupon changed 'England' to 'Freedom', and this change appeared in the book. It also appeared in Michael Balcon's film.

The following day, mid afternoon, I had a whim to take a stroll along the coastal path towards the onion meadow, the far boundary of Minack land. It had always been called the onion meadow, presumably because onions had been grown there, though no local could remember this. It had not been cultivated for many years, and it was now just brambles, couch grass and patches of gorse.

I reached it, then stood for a few minutes looking out to sea, to the long line of the Lizard which is like an outstretched arm along the eastern side of Mount's Bay. Below me, below the discarded meadows where the Magnificence daffodils which we used to grow commercially, and which still grow into bloom among the undergrowth, I stared at the two rocks call the Bucks, scene of the wrecks of many sailing ships in the nineteenth century; and there was a cormorant hunched on one of the rocks, unperturbed by the increasing, stirring sea, and the waves foaming against the rocks. A breeze, after a quiet day, was blowing up from the south, the clouds were grey and low, and hiding the horizon. It was going to be a dirty night, I said to myself.

I began to stroll back to the cottage, and I felt a certain elation that I was alone on this ancient, beautiful coast. It is at such moments that one feels another dimension to one's being which is impossible to experience where there are crowds and senseless noise. It is an experience of spiritual strength like that which monks of centuries past have aimed to achieve by cutting themselves off from the real world. I was alone with the jumble of my thoughts, and amongst that jumble hovered some of the men and women of *Went the Day Well*. Suddenly I saw a figure coming towards me, and as it came nearer, silhouetted against the dying light of the November afternoon, I saw it was a soldier. I was startled. It was as if a ghost in my thoughts had materialized into fact.

If one meets someone on a Cornish cliff when one is happy with one's solitude, there is an irritation that a momentary conversation has to take place. I curbed my irritation because the manner and appearance of the soldier impressed me. He was wearing a smart, parade-type of uniform, polished buttons on his tunic, and, at regulation angle, a beret with a badge on it.

'Surprising to see you here,' I said in a forced tone of welcome. 'Are you on some exercise?'

He was young, a toothbrush black moustache, an eager face.

'Oh, I'm not military,' he replied.

'What then are you?' I asked.

He was eager to talk. I did not have to ask any further questions.

'I'm walking the coastline,' he began, 'because there is a potential ecological disaster in Mount's Bay.'

'Oh,' I said, no longer irritated, 'what's that?'

'A quantity of cyanide containers have been swept off a cargo ship in the Channel, and they are being washed up on the coast west of Fowey.'

'Yes, but what's that got to do with you walking the cliff at this hour?'

The young man was so at ease. He was performing a task of very great importance, and he was glad to have an audience.

'I'm not military,' he began to explain, 'but we wear uniforms because it gives us prestige in some of the wild areas where we work.'

'What areas? What kind of work?'

'I belong,' he said, 'to the International Rescue Organization based in Florida. We are a highly trained, very compact organization which is on the alert to go anywhere where there is a major disaster, or where a major disaster threatens.'

'So why here?'

'These cyanide containers are potentially lethal to anyone who comes near them. They could wipe out the population of a Cornish town in a matter of minutes.'

'Why hasn't the public been notified?'

'That is part of our job. We are expected to solve the crisis before a warning is necessary.'

A curious remark, I found.

Then he went on.

'We have found thirty-two containers so far. Our

Florida base possesses special motorboats and a helicopter unit, but the helicopter unit was committed, so we flew in with only our motorboats. We decided to rely on the Royal Naval Station at Culdrose for a helicopter but they couldn't offer any help today, but tomorrow and the next day they will.'

'What about the vessel which was carrying the canisters?'

'We're trying to identify it. Our Intelligence Unit believe they have found out it comes from Korea. Next thing is to find how many canisters were lost. How many there are to find.'

'Do you have many working on this?'

'We are a unit of five on this job. All very highly trained. We went to the Armenian earthquake, to the Alaska oil pollution disaster, to the Aberdeen oil rig disaster . . . we go anywhere at a moment's notice, and bivouac anywhere. I'm on my way to meet the others in the unit who are searching the cliffs eastward.'

'A very fulfilling kind of job,' I said. 'How did you get it?'

'I was two years in the Royal Marines,' he said, 'then I joined the International Rescue Organization with the help of my father who held a senior position in it until he retired.'

It was now dusk, and I said goodbye, wishing him luck. I then hurriedly returned to the cottage, contacted my friend Douglas Williams, Penzance correspondent of national newspapers, and told him what had happened. He had heard no rumours of a potential cyanide disaster, though canisters of some kind had been washed up at some places on the coast.

'From what you say,' he then said, 'it may mean there is a giant cover-up going on.'

There was no cover-up.

There was no unit of the International Rescue Organization in the area. Nor did the Organization exist.

The soldier was a phantom of my mind, of *Went the Day Well*.

Not quite.

He was proved to be a soldier with imagination who was absent without leave.

X

A grey, miserable day with a foggy drizzle hiding the landscape, the Tater-du signal droning its metallic noise.

Jeannie would say, when we talked together about the future, that she was sure I would marry again within three years if something happened to her; and I would reply that such an idea was rubbish, but I would like her to marry again as soon as possible if something happened to me, and to a very rich man who would look after her.

'He would have to be prepared to stay here at Minack,' she would say, laughing. Always with Jeannie it was Minack, Minack, Minack.

It is my luck that all my life I have been content to be alone when need be. I do not have to fill vacancies in my mind by mixing in the company of people, any people, just for the sake of such company; and I see no value in staring at the television just to fill in the time. I prefer to rely upon the senses, my thoughts, music, books, when alone. Yet there is danger in this attitude. Suddenly I will find myself attacked by a spasm of depression, of inadequacy, of fear . . . and then it is that I need a girl to be hovering in the background to give me the illusion of a love affair.

I can weave such an illusion because from time to time a girl may cross Monty's Leap, walk up to the cottage, and knock at the door. She will have read the Minack Chronicles or else she would not have bothered to come. She therefore knows me, though I know nothing about her. It is a good start for me. I realize that she likes me, or at any rate on paper she likes me. Naturally this gives me confidence and if, after the first introductory remarks have been made, I sense that we are both on the same wavelength, a friendship can begin; and thus is born my illusion of a love affair.

I now can pretend I have a fantasy companion as I fuss about my daily business. Cherry no longer has to rely on me to open a tin of Turkey Treats, nor does the General and his harem have to wait for me to throw the seed into the escallonia restaurant, nor does the dancing gull on the porch glass have to dance or to knock for more than a few minutes before bread is thrown to him. Then when in the late afternoon a gale is blowing and rain is belching down and I groan, 'I must go and feed the donkeys,' my fantasy companion brightly says, 'Let me do it!'

Nor does time or distance interfere with the illusion of my love affair. My fantasy companion may travel and she will send me a postcard from far-off places, from San Francisco, Brisbane, Cape Town, the Falkland Islands, Vancouver, Salt Lake City, or maybe from somewhere in Britain, a postcard of Exeter Cathedral, for instance. My fantasy companion is imaginative and generous. A pipe may arrive in the post, a bundle of pens, a shirt, a jersey, a tea towel, dried flowers patterned within a picture frame, bath essence. I am, of course, looking for a reflection of Jeannie. A reflection of her enthusiasm, her sex appeal, her fun, her agelessness. I am seeking the adrenalin with which she used to excite me.

Meanwhile my fantasy companion haunts me as I tidy the cottage, wash up, and cook. It is when I cook that I have special pleasure in her company because I am being positive. I am showing off. I am doing something specially for her. Or so I pretend as I bring out the Prestige pressure cooker, and begin to prepare a dish for myself and my fantasy companion.

Some people are scared of pressure cookers. The modern ones are safer than a microwave, quicker, and the contents far more nutritious. True, a mishap can occasionally happen, but a mishap can always happen in any sphere of life. I had a mishap the other day. I was cooking a luscious vegetable soup in a pressure cooker which I had had for a long time, too long; and I had been foolish enough not to have checked the valve. Suddenly the valve broke loose with a hissing scream . . . and much of the luscious vegetable soup ended up on the ceiling. Don't be put off by such drama. It was my fault. It was as if I had failed to check the condition of the car tyres.

Anyhow, here is the recipe of the first dish I intend to share with my fantasy companion. It is called simply the Minack Fish Dish. I devised it myself. Cookery books gave me an inferiority complex for a long time, until I realized that the cookery authors were not divulging long-hidden secrets but, for the most part, were offering recipes of their own invention. So I became unafraid. My range is limited, but I am no longer inhibited from tossing into a dish anything that I fancy. Here is the recipe for the Minack Fish Dish:

I find the dish so tasty that if it were served to me in Claridge's restaurant, I would be inclined to send a note of congratulation to the chef. Don't take me too seriously and you will have to work out the quantities for yourself, I've had my Minack Fish Dish problems, but you won't go far wrong with the following:

It takes three minutes to cook if it is unfrozen lemon sole, five minutes if it is frozen cod or haddock. Into the pressure cooker goes the filleted fish, followed by half a pint of milk, salt and pepper. Then I am lavish with chopped parsley because I grow my own, keeping back some for the sauce. I am eccentric about other herbs. I ignore normality because, truthfully, I have never grasped the conventional way of using herbs. Hence I pop anything handy into my fish dish, pinches of basil, herbes de provence, and a bay leaf. Then I close the pressure cooker with its lid, and here comes a potential hiccup. I normally have an automatic timer, but irritatingly, they seem often to go wrong (probably because I have put them in water while washing the lid) but this means I have to watch the timing. Three minutes only, or five minutes . . . then the time is up, and the steam is released, the steam hissing its freedom. I open up the lid, and there is the tasty fish awaiting further treatment.

I have an open pan ready in which butter is simmering, and I pour a portion of fish-flavoured milk into the pan, followed by more chopped parsley with a spoonful of flour to thicken the sauce. All the time I am stirring with a wooden spoon until the sauce is smooth. Then comes the secret of the Minack Fish Dish. I pour into the pan milk-poached mushrooms, accompanied by a dollop of double cream. My mouth is watering as I write. My fantasy companion is enthusiastic.

There is another special dish, my version of Chicken à la King. When I met Jan, whom my mother mentioned in her letter, after her performance in Robert Sherwood's *Idiot's Delight* at the Lyric Theatre in Shaftesbury Avenue, we would often have supper in a little restaurant in Beak Street in Soho, called Albert, presided over by Albert Pessione; one of his specialities was Chicken à la King, and it was very cheap. How does one interpret two shillings and ninepence in today's language? Jan and I enjoyed it often, and here is my version, which I would prepare for my fantasy companion.

First I steam a chicken in the pressure cooker. Ten minutes per pound for a boiling fowl, eight minutes per pound for a roasting chicken.

I simmer in a pan mushrooms and onions. Usually a half pound of mushrooms and a couple of medium onions. But this varies according to the size of the chicken and, for that matter, according to my need.

Meanwhile I strip the flesh off the carcass, a messy job, piling it into a bowl.

I then pour in the chicken stock from the pressure cooker into the pan of mushrooms and onions, adding a tablespoon of flour, stirring all the time. I then add milk, and after more stirring I empty the bowl of chicken into the pan, stirring vigorously with a long-handled spoon (a small spoon is not strong enough). I add more flour, and more milk, until the contents become a soft mixture. Then finally comes the double cream, and more stirring. Already, of course, I had put salt and pepper into the pressure cooker before the steaming, along with my customary collection of herbs plus a fingernail-sized amount of pesto sauce.

I reckon that when the task has been completed I have ten normal helpings from a four-pound chicken, probably more. Thus, after taking the immediate requirement, I fill foil containers with it, and store in the freezer.

Indeed the freezer is my saviour. Since I live far from any shop, I force myself from time to time to have a cook-in. I make a number of casserole helpings, or bolognese sauce, or soups, and store them in the freezer. Thus I always have something, home-cooked, ready for supper at the end of the day, when I am in no mood for cooking.

There is a third special dish. Indeed it was the first dish I ever cooked in a pressure cooker, and it converted Jeannie into approving the pressure cooker, provided she never had to operate it herself. It involves a gammon, three or four pounds in weight. And what happens is as follows:

I soak the gammon in plain water for twelve hours, thereby easing away the over-salty flavour. I may leave it in water even longer if I have something else to do, or forget it is there. Then I place it in the pressure cooker, surrounded by any collection of vegetables that are available ... carrots, celery, an onion, parsley and so on, and of course I add the herbs. I fill the pressure cooker three quarters full with water, and the steaming begins. Allow twelve minutes per pound once the guiding valve appears, and so a three-pound gammon only takes thirty-six minutes before it is ready to serve.

There is a follow-up to this recipe. One carries on with cold gammon after the meal of hot gammon; and what I find especially delicious is lentil soup. I've had a weakness for lentil soup since I was a child, and gammon stock makes lentil soup to perfection. Pour in the lentils, making your own judgement as to how much, into the stock once the gammon itself has been removed, then steam it in conventional pressure cooker way for twenty minutes. A gourmet flavour as a result.

Such are the meals with which I would try to please my fantasy companion. I want, however, more from her than I can give her myself. I want her to jerk me out of a despondent mood. I want

her to surprise me, perhaps an unexpected visit
with a bottle of wine. I want her to stimulate me to
deal with tasks I have left undone. Indeed it is
stimulation that I most want from the company of
my fantasy companion.

My fantasy companion, however, does not stay
long. I imagine happy times with her, but I am
only a station where she stops for a while. She
brightens life for me, then continues her journey,
or returns to the base from where she set out. No
matter. Maybe another fantasy companion may
cross Monty's Leap, and knock at the door, and
give me the chance to offer her my pressure cooker
dishes. I have yet to imagine a fantasy companion
whom I will not always remember with happiness.

Christmas cards were now arriving and, after
one of the three postmen who call at Minack in
weekly shifts has dumped the envelopes, kept together by a rubber band, on to the porch table, I
have a relaxed time opening them. I do not hurry.
I walk over to my Regency desk where I keep a tin
of Down the Road tobacco, fill a pipe, and retreat
to the sofa, dislodge the rubber band, and begin
opening the envelopes. I want to savour every
moment.

It was now, however, that I wished I had a real-
life companion. Jeannie and I used to put down
the name of the sender of every card on a list as
soon as they arrived, and we were conscientious
about sending out cards of our own. Sometimes
they were photographs dealing with some aspect of
our lives, and at other times we would choose one

of Jeannie's delicate drawings. We were so conscientious that when a card arrived with no address, only the sender's name, it was my task to find the address. I used, at that time, to keep a card index of people who came here so that if the name was in the index, there was no problem. If it wasn't in the index, I proceeded to go through the letter files, looking for a letter that the Christmas card sender had previously sent to us. It was a mammoth task, as others find, and all normal work had to be suspended. Jeannie, meanwhile, was in charge of writing our names, adding messages, and writing the envelopes once the addresses were known. Tiresome though the effort may have been, there was a wonderful feeling of triumph when the last bundle of Christmas cards was pushed through the letter box. All this when Jeannie was at Minack.

I, on my own, tried to follow suit. I found it impossible. Indeed a lesson that I have learnt since Jeannie is that one should never try to do anything more than one can comfortably do. If you do more, then stress takes over. Hence I found that I had ruthlessly to discipline myself, and one of the casualties of such discipline has been the Christmas cards. I am sad about it because I love receiving such cards. I feel the warmth, the affection, the trouble and, for that matter, the expense. There is, however, a hiccup in not sending out cards. In January I receive letters from well-meaning people saying, 'We didn't hear from you at Christmas, I hope you are all right!'

A practical problem follows the arrival of the

cards as the pile mounts up. Who can help me pin them up on the cottage beams and arrange them elsewhere? I am vulnerable at Christmas, the same as others in similar circumstances; and I am inclined to over-react. When I see the ever-mounting pile of lovely Christmas cards, I will have one of those secret moments of despair, one of those moments when the raging knowledge of one's loss smashes you, and some Christmas of another year is irrationally remembered.

On this particular day as I sat opening the Christmas cards, I remembered a Christmas Day when a famous foreign correspondent of the *Daily Mail* called Jackie Broadbent came to stay; and made a remarkable prophecy, born of his knowledge of the international world. A few days before Christmas he had sent a telegram, asking if he could come for Christmas. It was surprising. We thought he was in Washington; he might have been anywhere. He was a worldwide observer of the political scene.

We had Jeannie's mother staying with us. A sweet, easy person to be with, she was in the spare room; and the only place we had for Jackie to stay was in the flower house on a camp bed upon which Jeannie's father had slept during the First World War. We sent a telegram back: 'Love to see you.'

Thus it was on Christmas morning that I heard from him the prophecy, and warning, that was to make that Christmas memorable:

I took Jackie his morning tea, and because there was frost in the wind, Jeannie had filled a thermos.

I carried it with a cup down the path and across to the flower house wondering whether, in this cold, Jackie had slept a wink. I opened the door and wished him a Happy Christmas, but there was no reply. The bedclothes were pulled up to his eyes and I thought he was asleep, and without trying to wake him I bent down and lit the paraffin stoves which stood by the door. I felt the heat suddenly emerging from them, and knowing the room would soon be warm, and that the tea would remain hot in the thermos, I decided to leave him. I opened the door.

'Come back!'

'Good heavens, Jackie, I thought you were asleep.'

I picked up the thermos, unscrewed the top and poured out the tea. 'Merry Christmas,' I said. Then I added, laughing, 'So you were wide awake all the time I was looking after your welfare, lighting the stoves!'

'Wide awake? I've been wide awake all night. What else do you expect a man to do lying on a bed of World War One, reminding him of the idiocy of the human race?'

Then he went on.

'Forty-five years ago men slept on this bed dreaming of the greatness of the British Empire, girls, drink, white supremacy, the glory of dying for a brave new world, contentment, riches, all the delusions that lead men to their end.'

'You *are* cheerful,' I said.

'I am so cheerful that I could dance,' and he kicked his legs up and down under the bedclothes.

'Listen,' he said, 'as I lay shivering in this bed I

heard the guns of Passchendaele. The primitive guns which could only kill a few at a time . . . and I saw the leaders of opinion in any country of the world, all are the same, politicians hiding behind generals, society groups manipulated by ambitious men and women. I saw them not only in this country, but in all countries. There they were, all desperately earnest in their fashion, intoxicated by a flag and a symbol, simple people elevated by luck to leadership of the rabble. All of them, both sides, were sincere in committing their faults or virtues . . . but . . . that generation which slept on beds like this one were only *toying* with war.'

'Obviously,' I said, 'despite the losses.'

'Ah,' he said, 'you're thinking about the Great Powers. I am not. They have their own histories to guide them and to steer them clear of trouble unless there is an accident.

'Mark my words . . .'

And now came the prophecy and the warning which made that Christmas memorable. The year was 1961:

'Mark my words . . . Russia will come to terms with America before long. They're safe. It's the juvenile governments I'm thinking of. No history to guide them, no Passchendaele to tell *them* of war. A nuclear bomb is a plaything in their primitive political struggles, a trivial ally to their shouts. Sooner or later the bomb will be the revolutionary weapon, the terrorist's weapon. That's what I was thinking about on this Passchendaele camp bed.'

Dear Jackie. He was a very special friend. He died three months later in mysterious circumstances.

That December as I sat opening the Christmas cards, the weather turned very cold, and in mid December two New Zealand friends from Christchurch and their English hosts had proposed a lunch party for which they would bring pasties.

A gale had been gathering strength all morning, and the clouds were low and grey, and the gale was coming from the north-east, and by midday it was bitterly cold, and it had begun to snow. I was not in the mood for a party, and I had work to do before my friends arrived, tidying up the cottage, that tiresome tidying which ends up by piling things out of sight in cupboards or in corners behind an armchair. A messy kind of tidying-up. I had completed my task by midday, and by that time the snow was swirling down as in an old-fashioned Christmas card, and I decided that such weather would warn off my friends, and I would be able to be snug on my own with Cherry, as the snow blanketed the land around Minack.

Not the case. My charming New Zealand friends and my English friends left their car at the top by the farm, and walked down the winding lane, thrilled that they were coming to Minack in a snowstorm. We had a happy time, played records, ate the pasties, and looked out of the window every now and again and said it was snowing harder than ever. The New Zealanders had recently been in Jerusalem, and one day they got friendly with an

Arab trader in the bazaar. The Arab became flirtingly interested in the very pretty New Zealand wife, and said humorously, 'I'll give one hundred camels for her!' They told me this story and I replied, 'I'll give ten thousand daffodil bulbs!' It was that kind of innocent happy party, as the snow fell around Minack. Then suddenly stopped.

Next morning I stayed an extra time in bed. I could see through the window from my bed that Oliver land was a patchy white. I expected it to be covered with snow, but during the night there had been a sudden thaw, and when I got up and went outside the air was balmy, the ground in slush and puddles. I was delighted. The day could now be normal.

The General appeared from the escallonia followed by a couple of his ladies, and no doubt they too were pleased that the day was going to be normal. I threw them a couple of handfuls of bird seed and peanuts, and the small birds hopped around trying to obtain their share; and up on the roof the Lager Louts started to bellow, and so I returned to the porch, collected slices of bread and threw them on the roof. A pair of magpies squawked, swooped, thought better of it, then swooped again, pinching some of the bread from under the beaks of the Lager Louts. I am baffled by the efficiency of the Magpie Intelligence Service. Not a magpie in sight yet one throws food to the other birds, and the magpies appear in seconds. If only the anti-terrorist intelligence service was as efficient, the terrorists would soon be defeated.

My next move was to see the donkeys.

'Here you are,' I said when I reached them, fighting with my fingers to tear open the top of a packet of tea biscuits which I had brought with me.

I stood beside them as they munched. Dignified Merlin, perky Susie. Huge Merlin, tiny Susie. Here were two representatives of a maligned, ill-treated race, living in the freedom which all seek. I looked at their crosses, Merlin's merging into his shaggy brown coat, Susie's black-pencil sharp against her grey thin coat. In this age that clamours for a logical explanation for every mystery, it is pleasant that no one has developed a logical explanation for the cross of a donkey. Nobody has tried to knock the traditional interpretation that all donkeys were blessed with the cross because Jesus chose a donkey to ride into Jerusalem. How refreshing! Donkeys, brutally treated and despised, retain a therapeutic quality which affects everyone who comes into contact with them, whether a child on a beach donkey, or all those who support donkey sanctuaries like Mrs Svendsen's famous Sanctuary at Sidmouth in Devon. There is no logical explanation because it is a spiritual quality which a donkey exudes, an indefinable awareness that a donkey is reflecting tragedy over the centuries, indomitable courage and the love which earned its cross in the beginning.

I left the donkeys, went back across Monty's Leap, paused for a moment to sniff the soft scent of the heliotrope, then on past the ancient surface well on my right, the blue door of the confusion room on my left and then, a jerk in my mood, I turned right through the gap which led to the Orlyt glasshouse.

I welcomed this normal day. I walked along the footwide path with the granite trough, two centuries old, on my right and the two stem-naked Peace rose bushes on my left, then on a few yards to the door of the flower house which housed the two freezers. I walked . . . then stopped in horror.

Three quarters of the Orlyt facing the wood was in smithereens. The weight of the snow, helped by the gale-force wind, had crushed the structure, smashing the glass into a multitude of jagged pieces. The side facing the lane was little better. The glass seemed to be intact but on looking more closely I saw that the supports had gone, and the glass roof was swaying dangerously. It was the end of the Orlyt. The day was no longer normal. I was in despair.

I returned to the cottage, sat down on the sofa, murmuring to myself, as if the words were prompted by Jeannie, 'Keep calm, keep calm.' A moment when I longed for a companion.

It was not the incident itself which was hitting me. The emotional state that I was in reflected the experiences of things past. The memory of the time, for instance, when the Orlyt was first erected, and Jeannie and I celebrated with a bottle of Moët Chandon and toasted the Orlyt's future; and how we then had our first disappointment. We were advised to grow a variety of sweet peas which would

flower in April, and we filled the Orlyt with eight
rows of them, each one hundred feet long. They
grew luxuriantly, a mass of green leaves on each
stem as they climbed up the attached strings ...
but none of them flowered. Not a single stem had
a bloom.

Two thousand tomato plants followed, and when
we harvested the tomatoes we labelled them 'Tomatoes Grown for Flavour', and both slogan and tomatoes were a great success. The following winter we
grew six thousand lettuces called Fortune, and they
grew plump and appetizingly green; and in early
April a wholesaler had one look at them, gave us a
contract price for the lot, and despatched them to
London.

Then there was the occasion concerning Jane of
A Drake at the Door. Jane had come to us when
she was fourteen years old, left a couple of years
later to go and work on Bryher Island in the Scillies
with her mother, moving to Tresco after her
mother died, where she worked in the famous
Tresco Gardens.

She came to stay with us for the Penzance Spring
Flower Show, bringing her entry for the Prince of
Wales's Cup with her, a collection of Carbineer
daffodils which she had to arrange on the morning
of the show. She placed them in water overnight
inside the Orlyt, but during the night a gale began
to blow and, by morning, even by our standards it
had become one of the worst we had ever known.
The Orlyt was swaying, Jane's entry beneath the
swaying.

I had to go into Penzance, and before I left I told Jane, and Jeannie, that on no account were they to risk going into the Orlyt while I was away. I was scared that, by opening the door, the flood of air might be enough to lift off the glass roof.

I went into Penzance, returned, and found Jane calmly in the packing shed preparing her entry, Jeannie beside her, and both laughing. Just as well that Jane had ignored me. She became the youngest person ever to win the Prince of Wales's Cup, the daffodil growers' most coveted trophy. These were memories of the enthusiasm and optimism of those days. The Orlyt, the now destroyed Orlyt, had been the mirror of that enthusiasm.

Two years after the erection of the Orlyt, we put up two more glasshouses, mobiles this time which we could move over two sites. Then a year or two later two more. We were intoxicated by our enthusiasm. We also had a Lloyds Bank manager who believed in us, and who was ready to finance us. Had it not been for Lloyds we would have folded up, and I would never have been able to write the Minack Chronicles, nor Jeannie her novels. The market climate was in our favour. Wholesalers were crying out for flowers and produce. Amateurs like ourselves did not have to compete with scientific knowledge that can deliver produce with the exactitude of a factory product, or with produce which is flown in from faraway countries. Jeannie and I acted as if we were growers in a conventional kitchen and flower garden but on a much larger scale. What fun we had despite the disappointments; and what satisfaction!

The fun, the disappointments lived all around us. The pride in sending away the first box of daffodils, the pride in placing perfect new potatoes on tissue paper at the bottom of a chip basket designed to take fourteen pounds, placing a cardboard cover on the top, weighing them soon after dawn, the sea beside us, silence but for the dawn chorus, tying up each chip basket in special fashion, loading them into the Land-Rover ... proud and satisfied that yesterday's diggings with a shovel were on the way to market.

There were other pleasures gained in the mobiles. We would have chrysanthemums in one, freesias in another, forget-me-nots, calendula, polyanthus in another; and always tomatoes in the summer. Jeannie used to disappear for a couple of hours and more, pinching out the tomato surplus growth, so therapeutic she would say ... and I would tick her off, saying that she only pinched out the tomatoes because it was a mindless task; and that instead she ought to be *using* her mind by drawing and painting, or pursuing the writing of another novel. No wonder I had once locked her in the spare room, bought as a chickenhouse, so that she was forced to write *Meet Me at the Savoy*.

I, too, was often guilty of such therapeutic mindlessness. I was serenely content to be on my hands and knees weeding the freesia pots, Jeannie weeding another row beside me. No thoughts at all. A blank, except for the pleasure of pulling with my fingers immature weeds from a freesia pot.

I sat on the sofa, remembering the words of a

local friend of mine, a one-time advertising executive who found life more rewarding growing violets and working part-time for local farmers and growers. He said to me one day soon after the mobiles had been erected, 'They'll become white elephants. You're thrilled about them now but just you wait!' It was more of a comment than a threat, and anyway we had no intention of being influenced by him. Then he added, 'Just look at me. I've a nice patch of violets. If a frost gets them, so bad. But I haven't lost any of my capital ... never deceive yourself that things are going so well that you can expand.'

I sat there on the sofa, Cherry having reached my lap in a roundabout way. She had jumped up on the end arm of the sofa close to the open fire, then made her way along the top of the sofa beneath the window, then down on the arm beside me, and thence on to my lap. Her presence helped me.

The destruction of the Orlyt was the final event in the saga of the glasshouses. The previous year had seen the great storm which battered Britain, and it battered the mobiles. They had been made useless. Numerous panes of glass had been smashed, littering the ground; and as the months passed more gales continued to smash more panes. I had been putting off making a decision as to what to do. Glasshouse growing had changed so radically that they would not be commercial even in good order; and in any case the cost of repairing them would be substantial. A lot of panes remained that could be saved but what to do with them?

Apparently no one wanted such panes; and what could I do about the smashed glass strewing the ground? These were decisions I had put off and put off. I had to face up to the fact that I must change my attitude. I had to find a solution before very long. The voice of my friend who only grew violets echoed in my mind: 'They'll become white elephants.'

My gloom eased when I consoled myself that I could do nothing until after Christmas. Therefore put it out of your mind, I said to myself, let the New Year take care of it ... and I now saw the whole affair in perspective.

This was a tin-pot worry compared with the worries besetting other people.

XI

Ten days to Christmas ... the same calendar date that the drama of the croft began two years before.

My old friends Walter Grose and Jack Cockram, our long-time farming neighbours, had retired, and a new tenant had taken over the farm. A change in attitude could be expected. A new modern approach to farming, and this new approach might show itself in a variety of ways, not always congenial. I, however, felt safe. Minack was a quarter of a mile away down the winding lane, a lane which Jeannie and I had built, turning it from a mud track on which no car was able to travel.

On one side of the lane was the two-acre rocky croft which had been undisturbed for as long as anyone could remember; and it was a haven for bird life, foxes and badgers. It was a natural conservation area, and provided a sense of isolation as one came down the land to Minack which people, apart from ourselves, cherished. Here was peace and naturalness, equivalent to a miniature rain forest. Moreover it was adjacent to our own nature reserve, Oliver land; and to the sign in memory of

Jeannie, reading 'A Place for Solitude'. But the croft did not belong to us. The croft came within the tenancy agreement of the new tenant.

On that December morning two years previously I heard the grinding, grating of a bulldozer up the lane, that terrible sound which has alarmed people the world over who live in beautiful, unspoilt places. The herald of destruction. What was the new tenant up to? I went up the lane to have a look, and found that the bulldozer was clawing an entrance to the croft. I was appalled. Was the peace of Minack about to be destroyed? A few days later I met the new tenant, found him putting up a barbed-wire fence close alongside the lane, and right down to Oliver land; and he was also about to put a metal farm gate where the bulldozer had made an entrance. He told me he was going to overwinter ten beef cattle in the croft, then send them to slaughter every April.

The prospect was repugnant but what right had I to object? The new tenant, a young man, had a living to make and, as a farmer, he had to get the most value out of his land. The land was his factory. He had to get maximum production. He could not afford to pander to those like myself who wanted to conserve nature. I could understand his point of view because I had behaved in the same way myself. Take the glasshouses. I had erected them to earn a living.

The beef cattle arrived a few days after Christmas, huge beasts which immediately began to trample and crush the croft. They had no shelter, and so they ranged the croft in all weathers, while the natural inhabitants of the croft, for their safety's sake, had to go elsewhere. I was watching a carbon copy, although in miniature, of the destruction of a rain forest. The croft became a symbol to me of what is happening elsewhere. What for? In this case to increase the beef mountain. In the case of the giant rain forests to satisfy the demands of over-population.

I was soon to discover the side effects of such destruction and again in miniature. A giant tractor was required to come down the winding lane every day with silage to feed the cattle; and when I saw the effect it had on the narrow lane, churning it into a quagmire, I thought of the multitude of tractors and bulldozers churning the rain forests. My imagination, now backed by reality, was horrified. So, also, were others horrified:

When visiting your beautiful nature reserve the other day, we were devastated to see the state of the croft. We believe this is the name of the adjacent field. It looked as though tanks or bulldozers had been over it. The winding lane, known to so many thousands by its title of one of your books, has also been desecrated, and in places is almost impossible to negotiate.

We are writing on behalf of those legions who have visited Minack over many years and who benefit in so many ways from the quiet peace and serenity of this beautiful oasis.

Considering the important status of Minack, made

internationally famous through your books, I hope
you will not mind one caveat in regard to what
was otherwise a most memorable visit. It concerns
the lane leading directly to your property. Just
where one reaches the point of no return, we suddenly came upon mud so deep and thick from
heavy farm machinery that my car swerved out of
control. You must have a vast number of readers
visiting you and the present condition of the lane
represents an accident just waiting to happen.

Always before when I have passed the farm and
begun walking down the winding lane I have had
a wonderful feeling of walking into your books, into a
world which is completely unspoilt, but oh, this last
time! It is obvious that whoever is responsible for
what can only be called vandalism is very insensitive.

For two winters I was to watch the cattle floun-
dering around the croft, and it was hurting to see
them standing within a few yards of Jeannie's
special sign; and I shuddered to think how Jeannie
would have felt about such temporary neighbours
destined for the slaughter house. They looked ami-
able creatures but, for a farmer, they were just
factory units.

A few weeks ago the situation was resolved, and
no cattle would flounder in the croft this Christmas; and the lane would no longer be a quagmire.
The landlord had made other arrangements with
the tenant, and the croft had been returned to its
original state as a conservation area alongside our
own nature reserve.

Eight days to Christmas ... I came out of the cottage in mid afternoon, a dark afternoon, low clouds, and saw a girl standing by Monty's Leap. I called out, 'Hello!' She remained still. I hesitated, then called, 'Come on up if you like!' She came walking up to the cottage, and stood beside me, very shy. She was Australian, twenty years old, and she came from a farm in Queensland with four thousand sheep, thirty miles from any town. She lived there, helping on the farm, with her mother and father, and her four sisters.

'I've read some of your books, and they made me want to come here. I walked along the coastal path, then turned back, and came round and down the winding lane.'

She continued to remain very still.

'How long are you over here?'

'I'm on a working holiday ... I decided to get away from my home because I wanted to look for experience to help develop my character.'

'Sounds very earnest.'

'Can you imagine what it is like living enclosed in a family miles from anywhere, and few opportunities to enlighten oneself?'

'I can imagine it,' I said, 'but I can imagine that it takes a hell of a lot of courage to break away, and go to places far, far away.'

Then I asked, 'Where are you staying?'

'I'm travelling on an agricultural scheme which gives the addresses of farms where I can stay. The one I'm staying with now is just outside Penzance. I go to a farm in Scotland for Christmas.'

'What is your name?'

'You will laugh!' and it was the first moment she seemed at ease. 'My family name is Casanova!'

I didn't laugh.

'What is your Christian name?'

'Anne.'

I asked no more questions.

'It's getting dark,' I said. 'Come inside the cottage and see what a seventeenth-century Cornish cottage looks like with all the twentieth-century mess in it – and after that I'll drive you back to Penzance. I've got shopping to do.'

'You won't mind?'

'Of course not.'

I drove with her to Newlyn, and bought carrots for the donkeys from Drew's the greengrocers, bringing her into the shop with me. Then I went on to the Cossins' newsagent shop, and bought tea biscuits, also for the donkeys, and postcards for the girl. The lady behind the counter, whom I knew well, looked at the girl and said how pretty she was. 'Is she staying long?' she asked, turning to me. 'Oh no,' I replied, 'we're on our way to the bus stop, and she's catching a bus to St Erth.'

We reached the bus stop.

'Goodbye,' I said, 'good luck!'

'Can I write to you?' she suddenly said urgently, as she was about to get out of the car. 'I'll want to write to you. I'll never forget today.'

'I would love you to write to me.'

She was never to do so.

Four days to Christmas . . . panic. The Christmas cards were in a mounting pile. I hadn't arranged any of them. I hadn't bought a Christmas tree, and I remembered that last year's tree light didn't work. I had only had time to send out a few cards, and these were left-over cards I had for announcing the publication of *The World of Minack*. I was in disarray. I needed a fantasy companion, to calm my emotions, organize me, give me encouragement, and just by her presence inspire me to get on with the work I had to do. Instead for the time being I had given up. I had flopped on to the sofa, staring into space, unable to begin any of the tasks I had to do, immobile like a car which refuses to start.

There was a collection of books, papers and an old diary or two, heaped untidily at the opposite end of the sofa to me. I picked up one of the diaries; it belonged to long ago, and I remembered putting it there a few weeks before as a reference for an article I was planning to write.

I began turning the pages, and suddenly there was a page of my handwriting, describing the first holiday I ever had with Jeannie. We were not married. It read:

> I stayed the night at the inn at Malpas, and met Jeannie at Truro station next day. Then we went to Lambe Creek House which Beakers Penrose had lent us, and we stayed until the following Tuesday when we went by bus to Newquay where I introduced Jeannie to Monkey [curious nickname for my mother] and Pops for the first time, and they loved her.

For the life of me I do not see myself ever being able to find a girl like her again. Slim, exquisitely pretty, and a perfect companion. She fits into every mood, and her gentleness smoothes away all troubles, and her zest for life makes everything so much brighter than when it is seen by oneself. She has such a delicate mind. It seizes the point however softly it might have been made. She is provocative, and men fall in love with her. She has a wide knowledge of public affairs, a knowledge of art and literature, and she is never at a loss in a conversation, and she has a delicious sense of humour. No wonder she is so popular with all those American correspondents who use the Savoy Hotel as their base.

At the end of that first holiday together I gave her a copy of my first book *Time Was Mine*. In it I wrote:

> So to remember Wild Wood;
> The swans of Lambe Creek;
> Ernie;
> The rowing boat across the Fal at Malpas;
> And one morning in a gale on the cliffs of
>   Trevelgue.

There was also a hardcover notebook in the pile, and I began thumbing through that as well. It was a notebook of quotations, and all had been written down by me before I was twenty years old. I had this thirst to gain experience of life, and I was not collecting that experience in the confined set in

which I moved. I had therefore become aware that
if there is any short cut to gain experience, it must
be through biographies, autobiographies, and novel-
ists like Proust, Balzac, Dostoevsky, Turgenev,
George Moore, Somerset Maugham, and all the
others who wrote about the complexities of minds
in real situations. I avoided surface books, those
whose object is to titillate, books which are written
just to help one pass the time. I just wanted, at the
age of twenty, to learn about life. Not that I think
my good intentions helped me very much. I never
seemed to learn the lessons I should have learnt.

Here are samples of the quotations I chose. The
first one is of my own invention. It amuses me:

> Youth have the years in front of them to fill with
> hope; but when the years have gone there is no
> place for hope to go.

> And if he would be beloved for himself he must
> cultivate an interesting attitude of mind, and take
> part in wider humanity, in dreams, hopes, aspira-
> tions and ideals not strictly his own, only his
> through sympathy with the lives of others.
>
> George Moore

> How often is not the prospect of future happiness
> sacrificed to one's impatient insistence upon an
> immediate gratification.
>
> Marcel Proust

> Our desires cut across one another's paths, and in
> this confused existence, it is but rarely that a piece

of good fortune coincides with the desire that clamoured for it.

Marcel Proust

A prolonged separation, in soothing rancour, sometimes revives friendships.

Marcel Proust

Don't run after a haycart which refuses to give a lift.

Hungarian Proverb

Read carefully and do not be satisfied with a superficial understanding of a book.

Marcus Aurelius

The only universal language is the language of tragedy, for the laughter of the west is not the laughter of the east, nor is the wit of the palace, the wit of the tenement house; but the pain of all the children of Adam is the same pain.

Unknown

Our use of literature mustn't be a seeking after entertainment or play, but an effort to come gloriously alive.

Ernest Raymond

Living in this studio in spite of my dissipations was not unserviceable to me. It developed the natural man, who educates himself, who allows his mind to grow and ripen under the sun and wind of modern life, in contradistinction to the university man who is fed upon the dust of ages, and after a formula which has been composed to suit the requirements of the average human being.

George Moore

Christmas Eve . . . panic over. Friends born from the Minack Chronicles called the day before, Aline and Mike Gardner and their son Michael, and they took charge. They took charge of the Christmas cards, and the pile began to diminish, and within two hours the task was completed. Beautiful cards bedecked the cottage, pinned along the beams, filling the window sills, edging books and picture frames, tops of furniture, everywhere were Christmas cards; cards with badgers, cards with a cat in the window, old-fashioned cards with snow scenes, with London and country scenes, cards with a donkey in a stable, cards with a robin, a card from David Wills who photographed the jacket of *The World of Minack*, a hilarious card created by himself of three cats singing 'Silent Night' together; and at the granite base, window-sized entrance to the cloam oven propped against two precious objects were other cards.

The precious objects? One came from Canterbury Cathedral, the other from our one-time home overlooking the finishing post of the Boat Race. The first was a chunk of grey stone, the original Caen stone of Canterbury Cathedral. A young girl visitor had brought it as a present, having found it while the walls of the cathedral were being repaired. The second was a chunk of red brick, a piece of the original Elizabethan cottage at Mortlake which, during a nostalgic passing visit a few years ago, I purloined from workmen who were knocking down a wall.

The cottage now looked festive. My worries were over. The Christmas tree I had bought from our local store at St Buryan was sparkling with its decorations in the porch. The peaceful time of Christmas was at hand.

A breeze had begun to simmer in the morning, changed into a wind, changed into a gale, changed into a roaring gale, and the local radio announced at one o'clock that a hundred miles per hour had been recorded at the Falmouth Coastguard Station.

Sometimes I feel that a gale is a temperamental being. Moods change ten times every five minutes. There is a sudden silence followed by a murmur, then a sound like a giant brush sweeping the cottage walls, then a flash of temper growing into a rage, the windows rattle, there is a banging at one end of the roof, everything earthbound is under threat, and the noise crescendos like two people have a blazing row ... and then there is a pause, a seeming reluctance at having displayed such anger, a shame, and there is this quiet, a catching of breath, and, for a few seconds you may think that the gale has tired of its rage. You are wrong.

I took it easy on Christmas Eve, stayed indoors. At one point I started to sort out a pile of papers, attempting to file them, and then I stopped. 'Hell,' I said to myself, 'it's Christmas!'

Cherry had gone out after lunch, and she had

not returned. It had begun to concern me. Her recovery, or so it seemed, had been complete. She had never looked better, and she behaved like a kitten, chasing odd bits of paper, playing with pens on my desk, holding me up by sitting on my manuscript, as she is doing at this moment, and doing silly things like finding a way to the top of the bookcase, but not finding a way back. Her black fur, tinged with the orange of Monty and Ambrose, was lush. I brushed it every morning, and she enjoyed it so much that she wanted it brushed before she had her breakfast. Her return to normality was my most stirring experience of the year, and restored my confidence that miracles can be achieved. But she was out, and I knew how the other cats of Minack used to go berserk when a gale is blowing. The noise, the mysterious behaviour of leaves, the sudden movements of anything strange on the ground, hypnotizes them, compelling them to remain with the excitement of the storm.

Late afternoon, and it was time for me to get ready to present the donkeys with their mincepies. I put on another jersey on top of the one I already wore, put on a mac, and collected the homemade mincepies which an admirer of Merlin and Susie had presented to me.

I turned the handle of the porch door, opened it, stepped forward, and my foot met something soft.

'Oh, Cherry,' I said instantly, 'I'm so glad you're back!'

But it wasn't Cherry.

It was a large bird . . . a cormorant!

I was so astonished that I didn't, for a moment, notice the General, a few yards away by the escallonia, who was plainly impatient for his Christmas Eve supper.

'Wait, General!' I called out.

The cormorant had moved away towards the pile of logs two or three yards away, shuffling, swaying, the efforts of a being trying to prove that mind can triumph over matter. Where had it come from? How much of the ocean had it covered, wings beating against the storm, in order to arrive at Minack on Christmas Eve in exhaustion?

I watched it clamber in ungainly fashion up the pile of logs. The light was failing, the storm increasing, the rain gushing. I watched it settle, not comfortably but out of necessity; and I decided I could do nothing for it at the moment, and that I had better give the General his supper, then go to Merlin and Susie with the mincepies. I could then concentrate my attention on the cormorant.

I turned back to the cottage, dipped a cup into the grain-filled tin, and tipped it into the escallonia restaurant. I then set out to see the donkeys.

In the beginning, when the mincepie ceremony first began, when Penny and Fred were the donkeys of Minack, the ceremony was held in the stable close to the cottage; and so it continued until Penny died, then Fred, then Jeannie. I changed the site of the ceremony, anyhow for the time being, to the shelter in Oliver land . . . Jeannie's shelter.

I set out along the lane, head down, forcing myself against the gale, rain tearing at my face. Monty's Leap was in a flood, and I had to jump across, failing to clear it, so that one foot splashed into the water. Then on past the spot where Oliver had his first Christmas dinner, coming out of his hiding place in the undergrowth where I had built him a miniature cabin, coming nervously out to the plate of turkey which Jeannie had left for him . . . the same spot where I was to find Ambrose. I reached the Solitude gate, clambered over the stile, then turned left into the shelter, and to two waiting donkeys.

'Happy Christmas!' I said jovially, self-consciously. 'Happy Christmas, donkeys!'

I popped a mincepie into Merlin's mouth, another into Susie's. They were delighted and they pushed their heads forward . . . more, more, more. I didn't rush. I dangled each mincepie in front of their noses, teasing them. The shelter's floor was layered with fresh straw, and I had taken the precaution in the morning of giving them a double ration of hay. There was plenty left. They would have a comfortable Christmas night while the storm raged, tummies filled . . . All the while I was thinking of the cormorant, and the whereabouts of Cherry. Thus I did not stay as long with the donkeys as I would normally have done.

I battered my way back, and found the cormorant where I had left it. It shuffled when it saw me, scared. But if it was to have a chance to survive I had to catch it and bring it in out of the storm. I remembered I had a large cardboard box, full of files, which I had pushed out of sight in a corner of the spare room; and I went and fetched it, removing the files. Then I collected a large kitchen cloth with which I could cover the box like a lid, once I had caught the cormorant . . . and that was the problem, how to catch it.

It was dark now, and I had to use a torch. I placed the torch on a rock, the beam not pointing directly at the cormorant but to the side . . . then I made my approach. It was not an easy task. I had to half climb the pile of logs to reach it, and then having done so, to clasp it firmly but not too firmly. I succeeded, and swiftly carried it to the box which I had left in the porch, gently depositing it inside, and covering the top with the kitchen cloth.

'There now,' I murmured, 'you can have a quiet time. I'll keep a watch. No one will disturb you.'

At that moment I heard a car arrive.

'Damn,' I said.

For the cormorant needed total quiet.

But they were dear friends who had arrived; and they came with presents and Christmas Eve jollity, and although they were only too anxious not to disturb the cormorant, there was the inevitable laughter. Strange, I find, how often that when one of our animals has been ill, critically ill, the longing to be alone with them has been thwarted by a visitor. It happened when Jeannie and I were desperate about the illness of Boris the drake. How we longed to be with him as he lay ill, but we were distracted by a boring sense of conventional politeness, to be with two visitors who hadn't a clue of what we were emotionally hiding. I will be tougher now. I have learnt the lesson. If anyone tries to usurp my love of Cherry, or Merlin, or Susie by occupying me in chat, I will gently tell them to run. Yet, I ask myself, what is it in my character that tempts me to yield to the tittle-tattle on such an occasion rather than adhering to the values which I know are true?

We had fun, my friends and I. We hadn't seen each other for a while and so there was news to catch up upon. They were the Edwards family of whom I have written about before in another of the Minack Chronicles. Don, the father, was a member of the pioneer team which designed the Concorde; David, a lecturer on English literary subjects, mainly based in Toulouse, and to whom I gave a copy of *The Way to Minack* when he was sixteen years old; and Joan, his mother, who, after retiring from being a schoolmistress, concentrated on being an artist . . . and she is now so well known that she has attracted gallery owners from all over the world. My friends left with cries of 'Happy Christmas! Happy New Year!' And the lights of their car beamed down the lane to Monty's Leap, then on and away past the Solitude gate, tracing a film of light up to the farm and beyond.

I went to have a look at my cormorant.

It lay slumped, quite still. Those summer moments when it stood on a rock, wings outstretched to dry, the sea churning, those long journeys skimming the waves, the dives, the underwater swimming, the grabbing of fish . . . they were over now, ending in a cardboard box at Minack on Christmas Eve.

I now could concentrate on looking for Cherry. I picked up my Survival torch, a torch that is two feet long which looks like a weapon, and *is* a weapon in America where the police sometimes use it as a truncheon. Where had Cherry gone? She had been away from the cottage for six hours, and I was now really worried. I went outside and up the little path to the bridge, dipping my head beneath the escallonia branches that covered the little path like an archway; and all the while I was calling out: 'Cherry! Cherry!'

I went back, flashing the torch at the porch, lighting up the Christmas tree which stood on a shelf beneath the window, then sweeping the light around the little garden; and after that I set out down the path to the stables, past the cherry tree, thinking she might have found shelter there. No sign. I had become frightened. I was remembering her two 'attacks', one in March, the other in July; and I began to imagine that she had had another one, and had floundered into the undergrowth, and was so hidden that I would never find her. I walked down to Monty's Leap, reached it, and realized it was in such high flood that she would never be able to jump it. But supposing she had tried to jump it and had been carried away in the stream? One can have such silly, scaring ideas in such a situation.

Back I went, and shone the light on the piles of

broken glass around the Orlyt, jagged piles sparkling in the light. I thought of the car. Perhaps she
was hiding under it. Again no sign. I shone the
torch all round the neighbouring area, and I
reached a state of despair. I needed a drink. I
returned to the cottage, poured myself a whisky,
and sat down on the sofa, miserable.

I had been there a few minutes when suddenly I
had an instinct to get up and go to the door. I
opened it . . . and there was Cherry.

'Oh, Cherry,' I said, so relieved, no chiding in
my tone. 'What worry you have caused me! And
on Christmas Eve too!'

She displayed no shame. She sauntered past me
into the cottage, and to the plate which was empty.
She looked up at me, an order in her attitude,
telling me to replenish the plate. I immediately
obeyed.

Christmas Day . . . I did not get up until midday,
nor did Cherry; and even then I did not properly
get up. I put on a dressing-gown and opened the
presents, reluctant as always to do so because of
my admiration of the paper they were wrapped in.
Such a waste, it seems, to rip the paper impatiently.
Then I spent the rest of the day on my own. Kind
people had asked me to go to this home and that
home, but I was happy on my own on Christmas
Day. I enjoy being solitary. I did not have to make
a jovial effort, wear a paper hat, pull crackers, all
very happy-making for most people, but not for
me. I had instead the soothing pleasure of Creation
around me. I walked around, saw the first green

bud of a daffodil, heard curlews calling, wished the
General and his ladies a happy Christmas, threw
crumbs to a robin, smelt the sweet scent of the
heliotrope, listened to the dancing gull on the porch
roof, no man-made sounds . . . peace.

I took the donkeys their presents in early afternoon. Admirers had sent them carrots and chocolate biscuits but I rationed them. I gave them each
a sample of the presents when I found them in the
field, and then I tricked them. I wanted them to
walk with me on the way to the honeysuckle
meadow, and so I kept the major part of the sample
in my pockets. Of course Merlin realized what I
had done, Susie too for that matter, and so they
followed me, Merlin nudging me in the back. I
reached the green gate at the entrance to the honeysuckle meadow and, to their delight, I handed them
one carrot after another, one chocolate biscuit after
another. A donkey Christmas party.

I went through the gate, walked up to the rickety
seat and sat down. Jeannie was with me, so too
Oliver and Ambrose. So too, in my mind, were
others of my friends. M. was there who carried the
little basket holding Ambrose that May early
evening, stooping to pick wild flowers to place in the
little basket; and so helping me to stem my sadness.

'You're sure Jeannie wouldn't be upset, me helping like this?' she had said at the time. 'You're
sure? I don't want to be an intruder.'

M. was similar to Jeannie. Effervescent, practical, generous, emotional, beautiful. I was at ease
with her.

'Jeannie would have loved you,' I replied.

I sat there on the rickety seat remembering the day I decided to put up the green gate. The doctor had come in the morning, and I had asked the usual hopeful questions, and received the usual hopeful replies ... but I knew the story was ending. She was still at home, still cheerful.

Hence I suggested to her we should have a trip to Falmouth, to the smithy which made gates. A week later the gate was delivered and Mike, my friend at the farm, installed it. Next morning Jeannie and I strolled slowly to have a look at it.

'Stop!' I said as Jeannie began to open it for the first time. 'We must open it together!'

XII

There had been a lull in medium communications about Jeannie since the autumn, but early in January I received a letter from a New Zealand medium. She said she wanted to tell me about a visitation she had had from Jeannie at Christmas. Her letter was vague but there was no doubt in her mind that the spirit of Jeannie had visited her. She said that spirits contacted her by making a ticking noise like that of a clock. There then ensued a conversation. In Jeannie's case, the medium explained that she was in bed at the time with a copy of my book *Jeannie* on the table beside her. Suddenly there came from the direction of the book a ticking noise which became louder and louder. I reached this point of her letter, intrigued as to what Jeannie was going to say to her. She said nothing; and the medium could only tell me that the spirit, in the form of the ticking, was a very friendly one, and that she was sure it was Jeannie.

Such a visitation story was not very satisfactory from my point of view. Clearly the medium believed it to be of some significance, otherwise she

would not have troubled to tell me. It was, however, one of those vague medium stories which
tantalize but have little substance; and the letter
had come at a time when I was in a nostalgic
mood, and tense. I was living through the anniversary time, the time from Christmas to 22 February,
when I am edgy, inclined to take offence, vulnerable, foolish, one of the concourse who remembers
vividly the dates of a past sadness. In this mood I
am inclined sometimes to let off steam. Indeed I
have always been inclined to let off steam, and
Jeannie would be the unfortunate recipient. She
knew from experience that the steam was only a
temporary jet, and all would soon be normal again.
Someone, however, who did not know me well
might take offence. I had therefore to be careful.
Yet how much better to let off steam than to sulk,
nurturing a grievance, real or imaginary. The problem is to whom can one let off steam, who realizes
it is only a jet? And, for that matter, who refrains
from escalating the incident by talking about it?
One of the great rarities of life is to know someone
to whom you can bare your soul, your emotions,
without the terror of it being repeated to others.

When I am in this edgy frame of mind, I can
turn to Cherry. I read somewhere that you must
always wait until you have a personal crisis before
you can call a friend a friend. Cherry is totally
dependent upon me; and she never fails to respond
when I need to be dependent on her. She is, like
Monty, like Lama, like Oliver, like Ambrose, the
repository of my secret thoughts whether they are

of happiness, or anger, or of depression. She is so gentle. She soothes.

She does not have the normal hunting instincts of a cat. She may pretend to hunt, watching a hole by the hour, or being perplexed by a mysterious movement in the undergrowth, but she never turns such patience into action. I have never known her catch a mouse. I have never known her catch a bird. The escallonia restaurant, for instance, is much frequented by small birds, in addition to the pheasants, but they hop around unafraid. Cherry passes them by, showing no interest. She is so small, so pretty with her mainly black fur, much thicker since her illness, her off-white paw, and the apricot colour of her chest, and of her underpants; and I love the way she will skip down the path, pause, turn on her back wriggling, thus displaying those apricot-coloured underpants.

I love the way her little face looks appealingly at me as I touch or stroke her, the way she opens her mouth a fraction as a gesture of thank you, sometimes accompanied by a tiny squeak. I love the way she arches her tail across her back so that it almost touches her head when I am about to place a dish on the floor for her. I love the way she finds unlikely places in the cottage to sleep. I love the way she will sit sphinx-like on the red and white tablecloth in the porch, hour upon hour, just contemplating. I look at her sometimes when I am in an edgy mood, and have a subconscious fear of what might happen to her if something happened to me. I am her only one. Minack is her kingdom.

It is understandable why I turn to her when I am in an edgy mood.

Steve from Camborne continued to come on a Saturday when I needed him, pursuing his tasks at hurricane speed; and he continued to wander around Minack cliffs in mid afternoon when his tasks were completed. On one such occasion he brought back alarming information.

He had arrived at eight in the morning as usual, and proceeded first to clean out the donkey house, then he brought a couple of loads of donkey manure for the garden, followed by vigorously clearing up the garden itself. He is so vigorous that sometimes the overwintering plants are in danger. I had planted myself several such overwintering plants in the early autumn, small plants, difficult to see; and Steve didn't see them.

'Very sorry,' he said, adding with a laugh, 'I'm no gardener, just a maintenance man!'

It didn't matter to me. A hurricane worker was far more important than a few autumn plants ... and during that day, Steve cut a pile of logs, roto-vated the ground where the Orlyt had once been, mended the punctured pipe to the donkeys' water trough, carried up bags of coal so that it would be easy for me to fetch from close to the cottage ... besides the other tasks I have already mentioned; and when he had his lunchtime sandwiches, he and I relaxed and, on this occasion, had a discussion about fox hunting. Fox hunting was in the news. Parliament was debating its future.

'The lesser of two evils,' was Steve's opinion,

Steve who had spent most of his life in the country-side.

Jeannie kept her father's First World War sword at hand in case the local hunt invaded Minack territory. She had the chance to use it only once although she wisely kept it sheathed in its case. Toffee-nosed members of the hunt came pounding down the lane, behaving as if they owned the place, to be met by a shouting Jeannie wielding her sword. They turned, and galloped away.

Nonetheless, anti-fox-hunting though I may be, I appreciate the point Steve made that it was the lesser of two evils. The farming community would continue to kill foxes whether or not hunting was legally banned; and they would do so in particularly horrendous ways. There is, for instance, the 'sport' of driving a Land-Rover around fields at night, headlights blazing, and the occupants shooting at any fox, or other small animal for that matter, which the headlights catch in view. There is no caring for a wounded fox. It is left to die in agony. I have also known shooting at cub time. I have known a litter of cubs die of starvation because the vixen had been shot. Then there is the poison which is baited to catch a fox, and the illegal trapping which goes on undetected. Foxes are defenceless against such methods. At least the hunt gives them a chance to get away. What is needed in practical terms is stringent control of the way the hunt is conducted. In any case if hunting is condemned for being a cruel sport, how does one assess the degree of cruelty that involves catching from a river bank a fish on a hook?

Steve gave me his alarming news when he was about to go home. He had gone for a walk, after his work here had finished, along the coastal path towards Carn Barges. On the way, however, he noticed at the bottom of our field a faint track which might have been a badger's track, leading from the coastal path along the top of our one-time cliff meadows.

'I had an instinct to follow it,' he said. 'Perhaps it is because I am a countryman that I sensed something.'

The track, he explained, was so slight that strands of brambles covered it at places, and at one spot he had to crawl on hands and knees beneath a huge bramble bush. I realized that the spot he described was by the gate which led down steps (all now covered by undergrowth) to the cliff meadows, and eventually to the rocks and the pool where we used to bathe. He pressed on and, about fifty yards further, he found an opening down a steep bank. He followed it . . . and the consequence was the alarming news which he had brought back with him.

When he reached the bottom of the steep bank, he came up against the massive undergrowth falling down to the rocks, and he could go no further. Then suddenly to his right he saw a gap, and through the gap he saw what seemed to be a cultivated small meadow. He pushed his way through the gap and, sure enough, there was this meadow of newly turned earth, and just below it, another such meadow of newly turned earth. From his description I guessed they were the two small meadows where we grew Magnificence daffodils, one of the earliest meadows to be picked; and considered by Jeannie and me to be so secret that once upon a time we even thought of having our ashes placed there. Those two meadows tucked away, surrounded by high undergrowth, were very special to us.

It was too late in the day for me to investigate, but I did so the following morning. As Steve had described, it was a track that only a man with a badger mind could take; and it took me twenty minutes of sometimes crawling to reach the two meadows concerned. Clearly they had recently been dug over, just as in our new-potato days the same meadows would have been dug over well in advance of planting the potato seed. I noticed, however, other aspects of the surrounding area which suggested to me that badger digging and badger baiting may have been responsible. I experienced twenty-four hours of rage that this could have been the case but then reason began to take charge. I had never known a badger sett in that part of the cliff, and the penalties resulting from badger digging and baiting are now so severe that they were very unlikely to be the cause.

Hence I now called in the police. Perhaps the meadows were an IRA arms dump, and the cliff being accessible from the sea this was feasible. For why should two meadows, totally hidden from sight, the track to them hidden from anyone except a true countryman like Steve, have been reopened out of the undergrowth? My theorizing was too melodramatic. The explanation, however, was just as sinister, just as mystifying. Cannabis was being grown in the meadows.

The two police officers who reported this to me had brought back a dead cannabis plant, a last year's plant, discarded to the side of the meadow.

'Heavens,' I said, 'so they were operating there last summer, and I hadn't a clue!'

Who could have known such meadows existed? Who would have thought it worth the hard work and risk? Had a member of a fishing-boat crew earmarked the cliff as a cannabis site? Or had someone earmarked it from the air? When was the work done? Implements had to be carried there. Was it done at night? Of one thing I was sure. No local person was involved. So who was? As I write these words I still don't know. The meadows are dormant now, but soon will come the time when the seedling plants will be planted out. The police have asked me to keep a watch. Bizarre that after years of picking daffodils from those meadows I will now be watching cannabis plants.

I was also at this time suffering from a niggling worry which was of my own making. In the first week of March last year, exactly a year before, I had accepted an invitation to speak at a dinner in London. It was now in a fortnight's time. Many have made the same kind of mistake, accepting an invitation which is so far ahead that one does not believe it will ever materialize. I had, therefore, this niggling feeling of disquiet, the disquiet of what to take with me, the disquiet of organizing the caring for Cherry, and the donkeys, and the Lager Louts, of the General and his ladies, of the little birds; and the disquiet of leaving the security of my citadel.

Meanwhile I was experiencing the glory of daffodil time, a time which used to be the most hectic period of the year, as we picked, bunched and despatched the boxes to market. In those days many of the meadows would have been bare of yellow by early March, and only the green foliage would be left; and the first daffodils we had picked and sent away would have been in dustbins. Not any more. The daffodils, as they swayed in the breeze, looked as if they were laughing, laughing that they were free, not to be sent away to be shown off in early morning markets, shown off in shops, pushed into vases, ending in dustbins. They were rejoicing because they were staying at home.

People came to admire them.

'Go anywhere, stand and stare,' I said to them.

I had my own way of enjoying such moments. A soft, hazy morning, and I would set off to wander. I would wander among the rows of regimented daffodils, and I would pause to look at daffodils that grew in haphazard places. Such haphazard daffodils are like old friends which you haven't seen for a year; and there is one such clump that was the cause of a minor crisis in our first spring at Minack.

The clump grew in a bank that borders Oliver land, across from the stable meadow of Minack;

and it grew on a neighbour's land. We had an eccentric, earthy Cornishman working for us at the time who, for some reason involving a family row dating back a few decades, was convinced that the bank where the clump grew belonged to him, and therefore the daffodils. Hence, one day when I was out, he went across, picked the daffodils, and brought them back in triumph as a present for Jeannie. Unfortunately my neighbour, who knew nothing of the background story, saw him do it, and thought he was stealing them on my behalf. I soothed my neighbour by giving him half a crown. The clump still thrives.

As I wandered, my mind wandered too. I had moved into the *QE 2* meadow where there are beds of Hollywood, Magnificence, Joseph Macleod, and Dutchmaster, long beds; each bed used to take half an hour to pick with Jeannie on one side, Joan, or Margaret the potter who lived at the end of our lane, on the other. I stood looking at them, but my mind was elsewhere. I was thinking of the girl who had crossed Monty's Leap the previous afternoon. She was in her twenties, fair, appealingly pretty in a natural way, with eyes that, when she looked at me, made me sense she had a story to tell. She had two friends with her, a mother and daughter. I had felt from the moment they arrived that we were all on the same wavelength which meant we felt at ease. I began to probe their background in my usual inquisitive way. They came from Glasgow.

The mother, one of those sensitive, giving people, who inevitably makes those they meet feel happier, had organized this special three-day trip to see Minack. Her daughter, who was soon to be married, worked in a bank, and it was enchanting to listen to her pride and excitement in her marriage plans.

The fair girl was a friend, and she stayed silent, a little out of it, as I talked and listened to the others. Then her turn came, and she had to cope with my inquisitiveness. The consequence of my inquisitiveness was surprising. My questions, in print, may sound too direct, but they were said gently.

'Where do you come from?'

'I come from Essex.'

'How then did you come to live in Glasgow?'

'I ran away from home.'

'That needed courage.'

'I ran away twice. The first time the police caught me. I was fifteen.'

'How about the second time?'

'I made sure that no one would ever know where I had gone. I headed north, sleeping in ditches, barns, anywhere . . . it wasn't very pleasant, but I felt free.'

Then came the surprise. I had sensed there was something special about her, an inner strength which permeated the impression she made on me. I did not, however, expect the answer she gave me when I asked her what she did now.

'I am a minister in the Church of Scotland,' she replied.

My immediate reaction was to cover up my surprise by making a banal remark.

'How *interesting*,' I said.

My banality withered away within a few minutes; and now as I stared at the daffodils in the *QE 2* field I was remembering her reply, made so naturally, to another question.

'What sort of work do you do?'

'It varies. All sorts. The past three nights I have been up all night with the dying.'

I could imagine the sympathy she gave to those people.

'Do you follow a counsellor's guidebook?'

'Oh no, one needs intuition, spontaneous understanding, one has to get round corners by instinct. I don't think I would ever feel sincere if I was following a guidebook.'

'And it helps that you have suffered yourself.'

'I think that to understand other people's suffering you must have suffered yourself.'

I left the *QE 2* field to continue my wandering, and I walked down the path to the white gate which opens on to the field where Fred of *A Donkey in the Meadow* was born, and through which runs the coastal path. On the left were several beds of daffodils, California peering through the undergrowth, and a large area of Obvallaris, sometimes called Tenby, which are miniature King Alfreds. On the right-hand side we planted the first daffodils we ever bought, but it was only when we harvested them that we found they were not commercial daffodils, and the seller had taken advantage of our ignorance.

I now took the coastal path, meadows of our

daffodils on either side. I shut my eyes, remembering the hectic periods of picking, loading the baskets in the Land-Rover, and driving back to the packing shed; and remembering autumn days when I used to cut down the undergrowth that had grown up over the meadows during the summer, charging along clinging to the Condor, the powerful handheld rotary mower. I remembered an early morning when I caught a man and a woman picking daffodils in a professional manner, with a large basketful already picked.

I now reached the onion meadow where I stood looking down on what we named the Merlin cliff meadows. We had gone for a walk with Fred and Merlin one morning soon after Merlin had arrived at Minack, and he broke away from us, and galloped down the track bordering the meadows, then came to a sudden stop, ears pricked, quivering with excitement. Merlin had seen a ship for the first time in his life. The *Scillonian* was passing by on her way to the Islands.

Here again was the scene of hard autumn work. The cliff meadows being too small for the Condor and too steep, I used the motor scythe slung over my shoulder. I was doubtful when I first saw it. It looked too heavy, too cumbersome, but the salesman played a trump card: 'The Mother Superior at the convent uses one!' It was a splendid instrument for clearing the meadows. I would stand sweeping the ground in the way of an old-fashioned scythe; and Jeannie would be helping me by gathering the undergrowth I had cut, and tossing it out of sight. We rejoiced when the task was completed, for there was the rewarding experience of seeing the meadows clean, ready for the daffodils whose roots would already be stirring, meadows which fell down to the sea like giant green stepping stones.

I returned to the cottage, and took the path that led to the hut in the wood where I used to write when Jeannie was with me, she staying around the cottage in case anyone arrived, and so keeping me undisturbed. Boris, the drake, had his hut also in the wood, and Jeannie had a small one where she wrote *Hotel Regina*. Boris's hut has been crushed by a fallen elm, and Jeannie's hut is now covered by ivy and brambles. My hut is intact, and opposite is a splendid magnolia, and around it, and around the grass beneath the ash trees, grow the sweet-scented Sunrise narcissi. I stood there for a while, remembering. A bramble-covered bank faced my hut, and on the other side was the wood meadow, the so-called Periquita meadow, which ran alongside the wood. I could see a patchy amount of Joseph Macleod growing there, and Golden Harvest, and a patch of Actea in bud but not yet in bloom.

I heard a car coming down the lane, so I went back to the cottage, and found a father and son from Luton who visited Minack every year. The son left us to go to look at Tater-du, and the father sat with me in the porch. He was once a merchant seaman, and was now a security officer. He brought up the occasion when the *QE 2* paid a second visit to Minack. The first time Captain Warwick was the captain, the second time Captain Hehir. He told me how he served on a Cunard cargo ship of which Captain Hehir was the then captain. The ship was sailing into New York when the Cunard flagship, the original *Queen Elizabeth*, passed close by. 'One day,' my friend said to Captain Hehir who was then very junior, 'you'll be captain of the *Queen Elizabeth*.' 'Not likely,' replied Captain Hehir. It was, of course, the second *Queen Elizabeth* of which he became captain, sailing her one summer's day close to Minack, then paying a personal visit, a few weeks later.

'How I envy you,' said my friend. 'Values don't count any more in my world. The sensitive ones are thought to be loony. I heard a blackbird singing last week, the first of the year. I told one of my colleagues. His reply? "I haven't the time to listen to all that bird singing."'

After they had gone, I continued my wandering, setting off for Oliver land. I had reached Monty's Leap when, on looking back, I saw the little black figure of Cherry following me. This was not what I wanted. No doubt she thought I was only on the way to feed the donkeys, and she often accompanied me on such a mission, but Cherry was not a cat to take on a long walk. I had learnt my lesson early on in her life. She would start off with me, then ruin my walk by disappearing into the undergrowth, and refusing to rejoin me. Thus I now turned back, cajoled her to follow me into the cottage, and rewarded her with a saucer of fish. Then I shut the door, and set off again.

I climbed the stile by the Solitude gate, and walked up the field to the blackthorn alley. By the time I reached it Merlin and Susie had joined me, galloping across the field and expecting carrots or biscuits which I didn't have. They pushed their noses into me, but they showed no ill-will, and they proceeded to follow me. I walked down the foot-wide muddy track, then along the wider path, on my left a forest of gorse sparkling with yellow petals, and on my right the home of the badgers. They had been very busy. All around their main mansion, sheltered under a spreading elderberry tree, the ground had been flattened by their activity. In the centre of the path an entrance had been enlarged, fresh earth scattered, torn-up grass and old bracken loose around it. This was nursery time. Deep underground, cubs had been born.

It was in this area that Jeannie and I once rescued a beagle which had been caught in a badger snare. Snares used to be placed across a well-worn badger track and badgers, accustomed to use it for decade upon decade, would suddenly find themselves caught by a thin circular wire. The consequences were horrible.

One night Jeannie and I were kept awake by a howling dog. The howls were persistent, so we got up and dressed, and went searching. We found the beagle a little way off from the path, and the wire was around its leg. I had brought wire cutters with me, and I cut the wire; and the beagle was so brave that it made no attempt to struggle. In its terror it might easily have tried to bite us. We carried it back to the cottage, put it in the car, and drove into Penzance. On the way we telephoned a sleepy vet, and he met us at the surgery. The loop of the wire was still fast around the beagle's leg and we had been unable to shift it. The vet performed the task, and the beagle was free. It was three o'clock in the morning.

The path now turned left, and a few yards further on was the Ambrose rock with the ancient granite gatepost leaning on the side of it. The Ambrose rock holds the secret wishes of very many people who have touched it. Jeannie would touch it though she did not tell me what she wished ... except on one occasion. Her five-year-old nephew was in hospital and very ill. So, too, was the little daughter of a reader, who was in the Great Ormond Street hospital in London. Jeannie wished ... and both were to make complete recoveries.

I now sat on the rock, my legs not reaching the ground, and I sat there musing, Merlin and Susie, heads down, searching for tasty grass in front of me. In the meadow on my right, King Alfred daffodils were peering through the undergrowth; and looking back towards the cottage, I could see a film of yellow in the meadows around it. The breeze was soft, gently blowing off the sea which was rippling a murmur. There were no ships on the horizon, and I remembered the years when there were always cargo ships in sight on their way to far-distant ports. The massive rocky sentinel of Carn Barges was beyond the moorland in front of me; and I saw again the figures of Jeannie and me standing there on a June morning, seeing Minack for the first time:

> Jeannie suddenly pointed inland. 'Look!' she said. 'There it is!'
>
> There was never any doubt in either of our minds. The small grey cottage a mile away, squat in the lonely landscape, surrounded by trees and
>
> edged into the side of a hill, became as if by magic the present and the future. It was as if a magician beside this ancient Carn had cast a spell upon us, so that we could touch the future as we could, at that moment, touch the Carn. There in the distance we could see our figures moving about our daily tasks, a thousand, thousand figures crisscrossing the untamed land, dissolving into each other, leaving a mist of excitement of our times to come.

Merlin and Susie had wandered off, back along the path, and I decided to follow them. They did not take the path back to the blackthorn alley, but turned left along the path which led to the green gate of the honeysuckle meadow. They then found a bramble bush with green leaves just beginning to sprout and halted beside it. I wandered on, and had just reached the green gate when I saw the General in front of me. Funny old General. His permanent home, which I never found, was somewhere in the brush-covered area on the way to Carn Barges. There was a track which I kept open opposite the green gate, and I had often seen him take it. He showed no surprise at seeing me. He had had a meal in the escallonia restaurant, and he was now on his way back to base. He was limping badly. 'What are we going to do about you, General?' I said. He limped away from me.

I did not go into the honeysuckle meadow, just leant over the gate. Snowdrops filled the bank behind the rickety seat. Ascania violets, the original Cornish violets, surrounded it in clumps. Primroses, celandines, and miniature daffodils hailed the memories of Jeannie, Oliver and Ambrose. I did not feel sad. I rejoiced. Here was a celebration of the life we had led at Minack. Penny, Fred, Monty, Lama were all in my mind at that moment. Penny who lies in the corner of the stable meadow, Fred in the bottom half of Oliver land, facing the lane, Lama in the orchard, her name chiselled into a flat rock . . . and Monty.

Merlin and Susie had now joined me, then passed me, and I followed. I followed them back to their favourite field, noting the divots the badgers had made in the grass of the path, looking for beetles. Then I crossed the field and went over the stile, and on down the lane; and as I walked I thought of the multitudes all over the world who are seeking happiness, seeking peace of mind, seeking a way of life of fulfilment . . . and prevented from gaining their desires by an everlasting mismanagement of the universe; and by vicious minorities. Decade after decade the pattern continues.

'Is there never going to be an age of happiness?' cries a character from H. G. Wells's *The Shape of Things to Come*.

Magic used to enhance people's lives. Wonderment, through innocence, stirred the emotions . . . but science is destroying magic and wonderment. No longer can a child gaze at a flower, and marvel at its beauty. He must be told how it flowers, how it scents. All things beautiful have to be analysed. Everything has to have a sensible explanation for its existence.

I reached Monty's Leap, and I paused. Here was magic, and no logic will ever dispel it.

Monty's Leap is a symbol, a beacon for all those who set out to achieve the impossible.

A DONKEY IN
THE MEADOW

Derek Tangye

In this engaging story, Derek Tangye describes how
Penny the donkey and her delectable foal, Fred, come
unexpectedly into his life at Minack. Fred's huge ears,
fluffy brown coat and tiny hooves rapidly capture the
hearts of all who meet him and the adventures of this
endearingly cheeky donkey are a source of constant mirth
and pleasure.

'Derek Tangye is unique for the enviable life he leads and
the enchanting beasts who share it'
Paul Gallico

JEANNIE:
A LOVE STORY

Derek Tangye

When Jeannie and Derek Tangye withdrew to a cliff-top flower farm in Cornwall, sophisticated London society protested, but an even wider circle was enriched by the enchanted life which they shared and which Derek recorded in the *Minack Chronicles*. Jeannie died in 1986, and, in tribute to her extraordinary personality, her husband has written this portrait of their marriage. All the delight of the *Minack Chronicles* is here – the daffodils, the donkeys and the Cornish magic. And all the fizzle and pop of champagne days at the Savoy is captured as Jeannie dazzles admirers from Danny Kaye to Christian Dior.

THE WORLD OF MINACK

Derek Tangye

The World of Minack reflects the years Derek Tangye spent at Minack with his wife Jeannie before she died in 1986. It is a selection of favourite passages, many of them chosen by readers, from sixteen of the Minack Chronicles. With a special introduction, photographs and line drawings by Jeannie, some published here for the first time, it delivers a glorious celebration of a way of life that has been an inspiration to generations of readers.

GREAT MINACK
STORIES
Derek Tangye

Great Minack Stories contains three highly-acclaimed
volumes of Derek Tangye's memoirs: *The Way to Minack*,
A Cornish Summer and *A Cottage on a Cliff*. They combine
to tell the unique, touching and highly rewarding story of
how he and his wife Jeannie turned an implausible dream
into an idyllic reality.

Always yearning to 'get away from it all', Derek and
Jeannie left their hectic life in London for the peace and
tranquillity of a flower farm in Cornwall.

These memoirs highlight the contrasts and trace the
pleasures and pitfalls of both ways of life: the fascinating
people from the bright lights – Gertrude Lawrence, Alec
Waugh, A. P. Herbert, Kim Philby, Harold Macmillan
and Aneurin Bevin – and the enchanting Cornish years
that brought them closer to nature and to a deeper,
lasting joy.

SOMEWHERE A CAT IS WAITING

Derek Tangye

Derek Tangye's fascinating tales of life at Minack, his flower-farm on the rugged Cornish coast, are known and loved all over the world. Now three of his most famous books, *A Cat in the Window*, *Lama* and *A Cat Affair* have been revised and abridged to tell the whole enchanting story of the four cats who have shared his idyll.

Beginning with Monty, the lordly ginger tom who, as a kitten, turned Derek Tangye from cat-hater into cat-lover, he progresses to Lama, the little black waif who came to the door of Minack in a storm, and finally to Ambrose and Oliver, the inseparable duo who determined to install themselves firmly in the Tangye's favour. Here, for the first time, the cats of Minack are all together in one volume, superbly illustrated with photographs that show the full beauty of Derek and Jean Tangye's very special country world.

☐	A Gull on the Roof	Derek Tangye	£3.99
☐	A Cat in the Window	Derek Tangye	£3.99
☐	A Drake at the Door	Derek Tangye	£2.99
☐	A Donkey in the Meadow	Derek Tangye	£3.50
☐	Lama (illustrated)	Derek Tangye	£3.50
☐	Jeannie	Derek Tangye	£4.50
☐	The World of Minack	Derek Tangye	£4.99

Warner now offers an exciting range of quality titles by both established and new authors. All of the books in this series are available from:

Little, Brown and Company (UK) Limited,
P.O. Box 11,
Falmouth,
Cornwall TR10 9EN.

Alternatively you may fax your order to the above address. Fax No. 0326 376423.

Payments can be made as follows: cheque, postal order (payable to Little, Brown and Company) or by credit cards, Visa/Access. Do not send cash or currency. UK customers and B.F.P.O. please allow £1.00 for postage and packing for the first book, plus 50p for the second book, plus 30p for each additional book up to a maximum charge of £3.00 (7 books plus).

Overseas customers including Ireland, please allow £2.00 for the first book plus £1.00 for the second book, plus 50p for each additional book.

NAME (Block Letters)...

....

ADDRESS ....

....

....

☐ I enclose my remittance for _____

☐ I wish to pay by Access/Visa Card

Number ⬚⬚⬚⬚⬚⬚⬚⬚⬚⬚⬚⬚⬚⬚⬚⬚

Card Expiry Date ⬚⬚⬚⬚